# Year 6 Grammar, Punctuation & Spelling

# 10-Minute Tests

# 2023 SATs-Style Practice Papers

KS2 English ~ Ages 10-11

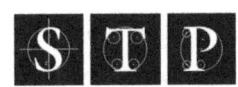

## Also By STP Books

### 2,000 Spelling Words Collection

### KS2 & KS3 Grammar, Punctuation & Spelling Workbooks

### Year 6 SATs English Practice Papers

Published by STP Books
An imprint of Swot Tots Publishing Ltd
124 City Road
London EC1V 2NX

www.swottotspublishing.com

Text, design, and layout © Swot Tots Publishing Ltd. First published 2024.

Swot Tots Publishing Ltd have asserted their moral right under the Copyright, Designs and Patents Act, 1988, to be identified as the author of this work.

All rights reserved. Without limiting the rights under copyright reserved above, no part of this publication may be reproduced, stored in a retrieval system, or transmitted in any form or by any means electronic, mechanical, photocopying, printing, recording, or otherwise without either the prior permission of the publishers or a licence permitting restricted copying in the United Kingdom issued by the Copyright Licensing Agency Limited, Hay's Galleria, Shackleton House, 4 Battle Bridge Lane, London SE1 2HX.

Typeset, cover design, and inside concept design by Swot Tots Publishing Ltd.

British Library Cataloguing-in-Publication Data. A catalogue record for this book is available from the British Library.

ISBN 978-1-912956-46-3

# CONTENTS

**About This Book & How To Use It**    4
**Notes for Students**    4

## Group 1
1.A Grammar & Punctuation Test    5
1.A Spelling Test    7

1.B Grammar & Punctuation Test    8
1.B Spelling Test    10

1.C Grammar & Punctuation Test    11
1.C Spelling Test    13

1.D Grammar & Punctuation Test    14
1.D Spelling Test    16

1.E Grammar & Punctuation Test    17
1.E Spelling Test    19

## Group 2
2.A Grammar & Punctuation Test    20
2.A Spelling Test    22

2.B Grammar & Punctuation Test    23
2.B Spelling Test    25

2.C Grammar & Punctuation Test    26
2.C Spelling Test    28

2.D Grammar & Punctuation Test    29
2.D Spelling Test    31

2.E Grammar & Punctuation Test    32
2.E Spelling Test    34

## Group 3
3.A Grammar & Punctuation Test    35
3.A Spelling Test    37

3.B Grammar & Punctuation Test    38
3.B Spelling Test    40

3.C Grammar & Punctuation Test    41
3.C Spelling Test    43

3.D Grammar & Punctuation Test    44
3.D Spelling Test    46

3.E Grammar & Punctuation Test    47
3.E Spelling Test    49

## Student Progress Chart    50

## Grammar & Punctuation Tests
Administration & Marking Guidelines    52
Answers    53

## Spelling Tests
Administration & Marking Guidelines    57
Transcripts    59

## 200 Spelling Words, Parts of Speech & Definitions    67

# About This Book

Designed to help **Year 6** students sharpen their English skills in the run-up to the SATs exams, this book contains **30 bite-size** **10-Minute Grammar, Punctuation and Spelling Tests**.

As all the Grammar & Punctuation Tests are **modelled on the actual 2023 KS2 SATs English Paper 1**, each test provides students with **up-to-date realistic exam practice**.

Similarly, as the Spelling Tests **target all the government spellings for Years 5 & 6**, the Tests **ensure students cover all 100 spellings** before the exams. The Spelling Tests also **target an additional 50 words** that students can find challenging. All the Spelling Tests in this book follow the format of the KS2 SATs English Paper 2.

**Each test** — whether focused on Grammar & Punctuation or Spelling — **is made up of 10 questions**.

We have provided **Notes for Students** below to give them an overview of the tests and how they work PLUS **a Progress Chart** on p. 50 for students to record their results as they advance through the tests.

At the end of the book, parents and teachers will find
- **All the answers** for the Grammar & Punctuation Tests along with Administration & Marking Guidelines
- **All the materials** you need to give and mark the Spelling Tests, including the Tests Transcripts
- **An additional revision tool**: a list of all **200 KS2 statutory spelling words** + parts of speech + definitions

# How To Use It

All the tests are **self-contained**, so they can be worked through in **any order**. However, we do recommend that
- Students **complete a whole group** before moving on to the next to avoid the possibility of doing two tests in succession where the types of questions are similar
- Students **work through ALL the Spelling Tests** since the government **words for Years 5 & 6 are distributed across all 15 tests** in this book
- Adults first consult the Administration & Marking Guidelines sections since they contain **suggestions that aim to help you maximise the usefulness of this book** to your children

## Notes for Students

### Doing the Grammar & Punctuation Tests

- Each Grammar & Punctuation Test is made up of 10 questions for you to ANSWER in DIFFERENT WAYS.
- Each question heading will make it clear to you what kind of answer is needed e.g. ticking a box, circling a word, writing a short answer.
- Each correct answer is worth 1 mark unless your parent or teacher decides otherwise.
- You should try to finish each test within 10 minutes unless your parent or teacher tells you otherwise.

### Doing the Spelling Tests

- Each Spelling Test is made up of 10 sentences.
- In each sentence, there is a BLANK SPACE for you to fill in with the ONE WORD that is MISSING from the sentence.
- You will need to get someone to READ OUT the missing words for you from the transcripts in this book.
- You should try to finish each test within 10 minutes unless your parent or teacher tells you otherwise.

### Good Luck!!

## GROUP 1 ~ Grammar & Punctuation Test A

1. **Tick ONE BOX** to show which sentence is a **command**.

   Tomorrow we are visiting our local library. ☐

   You can borrow up to three books if you like. ☐

   If you prefer, you could borrow five comics instead. ☐

   Make sure you bring your library card with you. ☐

   1 mark

2. **Tick ONE BOX** in each row to show if the sentence is an **exclamation** or a **question**.

   | SENTENCE | Exclamation | Question |
   |---|---|---|
   | What a fabulous costume you have | | |
   | What an unsatisfying end to the mystery | | |
   | What has happened to her bicycle | | |
   | What song were they best known for | | |

   1 mark

3. Draw a line to connect each word to a **suffix** to make four different words. You may use each **suffix** only once.

   | Word | Suffix |
   |---|---|
   | fright | ing |
   | laugh | ful |
   | king | ness |
   | dark | dom |

   1 mark

4. Insert a **comma** in the correct place in the following sentence.

   Cinderella spent her time dusting shelves polishing the silver and cooking meals.

   1 mark

5. **Tick ONE BOX** to show which pair of words are **antonyms**.

   market    supermarket    ☐

   natural   unnatural      ☐

   exist     coexist        ☐

   do        redo           ☐

   1 mark

5

**6.** Circle one word in each underlined pair to complete the sentences below in **Standard English**.

Did your new phone cost much / many more than your last one?

"This door handle feels a bit loose / lose," Jai said.

I want to go out to / too, but I haven't finished tidying up yet.

1 mark

**7.** Tick ONE BOX to identify the sentence that shows Maria is **most likely** to be delighted.

Maria should be delighted with her present. ☐
Maria might be delighted with her present. ☐
Maria may be delighted with her present. ☐
Maria will be delighted with her present. ☐

1 mark

**8.** Insert a pair of **brackets** in the correct place in the following sentence.

Becca whose favourite colour is purple has decided to plant lavender, hyacinths and foxgloves in her garden.

1 mark

**9.** Tick ONE BOX to show which sentence is the **most formal**.

Neil decided it was the right time to go to Chicago. ☐
The time had come for Neil to leave for Chicago. ☐
It was critical that Neil depart and travel to Chicago that day. ☐
It was time for Neil to hit the road and head to Chicago. ☐

1 mark

**10.** Circle two words that are **synonyms** of each other in the following sentence.

Our plan to deceive our enemies backfired; we discovered a disloyal soldier had been paid to betray us.

1 mark

*End of Grammar & Punctuation Test 1A ~ Now check your answers on p. 53!*

## GROUP 1 ~ Spelling Test A

1. Kim finds having more than one digital _____ annoying.  1 mark

2. "It is a _____ to meet you, sir," said Dr Watson.  1 mark

3. Greenleaf, the elf, decided to _____ Sir Tristram on his quest.  1 mark

4. "I can't get a _____ answer out of Ola," grumbled her brother.  1 mark

5. Can you guess what the expression 'to _____ on' means?  1 mark

6. Some insects _____ with each other by producing noises.  1 mark

7. Lorenzo always finds a good _____ in the sales.  1 mark

8. When did you first learn about the solar _____?  1 mark

9. "This street seems _____. Have we been here before?" asked Lola.  1 mark

10. I would love to go back in time to visit the first ever _____.  1 mark

### End of Spelling Test 1A ~ Now check your answers!

## GROUP 1 ~ Grammar & Punctuation Test B

**1.** **Tick ONE BOX** to show which sentence is punctuated correctly.

Professor Schmidt, who is the brains behind the discovery, is quite talkative. ☐

Professor Schmidt who, is the brains behind the discovery, is quite talkative. ☐

Professor Schmidt who is the brains behind the discovery, is quite talkative. ☐

Professor Schmidt, who is the brains behind the discovery is quite talkative. ☐

1 mark

**2.** Insert a **colon** in the correct place in the following sentence.

Our neighbours are very inconsiderate they constantly play loud music.

1 mark

**3.** **Tick ONE BOX** to show which sentence uses the word <u>face</u> as a **verb**.

His <u>face</u> had a healthy glow after his jog. ☐

The west <u>face</u> of the building was in shadows. ☐

Sometimes all you need is to see a friendly <u>face</u>. ☐

I can't <u>face</u> another bowl of soup for supper. ☐

1 mark

**4.** Rewrite the verbs that are underlined below so that they are in the **simple past**.

Tia often <u>makes</u> cards that she <u>sends</u> to her friends.

[_____]  [_____]

1 mark

**5.** **Tick ONE BOX** to show which sentence is the **most formal**.

Hal grabbed a sarnie coz he had the munchies. ☐

Hal purchased a club sandwich since he was famished. ☐

Hal bought a BLT because he was starving. ☐

Hal got a sandwich seeing as he was really hungry. ☐

1 mark

6. Insert **inverted commas** in the correct place in the following sentence.

   Have you found your shoes ? Kim asked .  1 mark

7. **Tick ONE BOX** to show which option completes the sentence using the **present progressive**.

   Pablo _____ the train timetable.

   is checking ☐
   shall check ☐
   has checked ☐
   was checking ☐  1 mark

8. **Tick ONE BOX** in each row to show if the apostrophe is used for **possession** or **contraction**.

   | SENTENCE | Possession | Contraction |
   | --- | --- | --- |
   | We're looking forward to our trip to Wales. | | |
   | The pirates' cutlasses glinted in the moonlight. | | |
   | My classmate's sister is our head girl. | | |

   1 mark

9. Replace the underlined word or words in the passage below with the correct **pronouns**.

   Lisa and Fred had planned to go hiking at the weekend. However, Fred
   [          ]
   
   sprained an ankle so Lisa and Fred couldn't go after all.
   [          ]  1 mark

10. **Tick ONE BOX** to show which sentence uses **tense** correctly.

    When Debora visited her uncle, she is clearing out his garage. ☐
    The plumber is fixing the leaky pipe before he checked the boiler. ☐
    Tomas eats his pasta while Sandrine drank her smoothie. ☐
    Jill is happy that all her friends have managed to come. ☐  1 mark

**End of Grammar & Punctuation Test 1B ~ Now check your answers on p. 53!**

# GROUP 1 ~ Spelling Test B

1. Palm trees had been planted at _____ intervals along the beach.  1 mark

2. He felt _____ as he walked onto the stage.  1 mark

3. Have you tried to live without the _____ of a smart phone?  1 mark

4. Serena's favourite dish used to be _____ lasagne.  1 mark

5. Terrified by the giants, the villagers were _____ to escape.  1 mark

6. He never likes the _____; it's either too hot or too cold.  1 mark

7. A flash of _____ suddenly lit up the dark room.  1 mark

8. The word '_____' is a synonym for 'group', 'class', or 'set'.  1 mark

9. Based on its title, that film is _____ a thriller.  1 mark

10. "Are many _____ spoken in Indonesia?" asked Layla.  1 mark

**End of Spelling Test 1B ~ Now check your answers!**

## GROUP 1 ~ Grammar & Punctuation Test C

1. Form the **antonym** of each word by adding a **prefix** to it. Use a different prefix each time.

   _____ continue

   _____ legal

   _____ behave

   1 mark

2. **Tick ONE BOX** in each row to show if the underlined word is a **verb**, a **noun** or an **adjective**.

   | SENTENCE | Verb | Noun | Adjective |
   |---|---|---|---|
   | She wrote a play to dramatize an important issue. | | | |
   | Her drama was performed at our local theatre. | | | |
   | I thought the ending was very dramatic. | | | |

   1 mark

3. Insert a **dash** in the correct place in the following sentence.

   Ben's old laptop is useless its screen is cracked and the battery only lasts ten minutes.

   1 mark

4. Circle the **subject** of the following sentence.

   Alicia found a hedgehog in the garden.

   1 mark

5. Show which **sentences** have been punctuated correctly. **Tick AS MANY BOXES** as you need to.

   Can Ted watch TV when he has taken out the rubbish?   ☐

   Ted can watch TV if he has taken out the rubbish?   ☐

   When Ted has taken out the rubbish, he can watch TV?   ☐

   If Ted takes out the rubbish, can he watch TV?   ☐

   1 mark

11

**6.** Insert a **pair of dashes** in the correct place in the following sentence.

Reg was beyond furious I'm not exaggerating about his new car breaking down.

1 mark

**7.** Circle the **relative pronoun** in each of the following sentences.

Sir Percy, who was in a bad mood, tapped his foot loudly.

His younger sister, Lady Viola, was yelling, which he found annoying.

"Why does Galahad's friend, whom we've never met, want to visit us?" she complained.

1 mark

**8.** Insert a **comma** after the **fronted adverbial** in each of the following sentences.

Irritatingly for Harry and I we missed the beginning of the show.

Soon after lunch the strange noises began.

1 mark

**9.** Insert one **apostrophe** in the correct place in the following sentence.

The ancient Egyptian goddess Isis features on many tombs walls.

1 mark

**10. Tick ONE BOX** to show which sentence is punctuated correctly.

| | |
|---|---|
| Lucy delivered the astounding news in her usual matter-of-fact-way. | ☐ |
| Lucy delivered the astounding news in her usual-matter-of-fact way. | ☐ |
| Lucy delivered the astounding news in her usual matter-of-fact way. | ☐ |
| Lucy delivered the astounding news in her usual matter-of fact way. | ☐ |

1 mark

**End of Grammar & Punctuation Test 1C ~ Now check your answers on p. 53!**

## GROUP 1 ~ Spelling Test C

1. I have no idea what my exact _____ is.  1 mark

2. Darren is _____ to learn how to make pastry from scratch.  1 mark

3. A _____ review of the company has been ordered.  1 mark

4. Loads of my friends have their birthdays in _____.  1 mark

5. "Don't you DARE _____ me!" hissed the witch.  1 mark

6. The members of the _____ argued bitterly for hours.  1 mark

7. The archaeologist took _____ care with the glass statuette.  1 mark

8. On _____, how much food does a horse eat a day?  1 mark

9. By _____, his aunt is a data scientist.  1 mark

10. "How SIMPLY _____ to see you, darling!" drawled the countess.  1 mark

### End of Spelling Test 1C ~ Now check your answers!

# GROUP 1 ~ Grammar & Punctuation Test D

**1.** Show what the **exclamation mark** could tell you about the following sentence. **Tick AS MANY BOXES** as you need to.

"What a wonderful surprise!"

It shows that the person is asking a question. ☐

It shows that the person is not speaking quietly. ☐

It shows that the person is not interested in the surprise. ☐

It shows that the person has definite feelings about the surprise. ☐

*1 mark*

**2.** Circle the **possessive pronoun** in the following sentence.

I had to ask to use the neighbours' printer as ours was out of ink.   *1 mark*

**3.** Using the boxes given, write the **contracted forms** of the underlined words.

You <u>must not</u> worry about having broken those plates;

[ ]

<u>it is</u> fine, really.

[ ]

*1 mark*

**4.** Underline the **relative clause** in the following sentence.

The dull painting which hangs in the hall was bought by Arnie in Budapest.   *1 mark*

**5.** Tick **ONE BOX** to show what the underlined words in the sentence below are called.

<u>As the knight approached the cave,</u> the ground began to shake.

a subordinate clause ☐

a main clause ☐

a noun phrase ☐

an extended noun phrase ☐

*1 mark*

14

6. **Tick TWO BOXES** to show which sentences contain a **preposition**.

   The fast train was very crowded. ☐

   Many passengers were standing. ☐

   There were luggage racks above us. ☐

   However, we couldn't use them. ☐

   They were full of other people's bags. ☐

   *1 mark*

7. How does the position of the **comma** change the meanings of the following sentences?

   (A) While Mary loves the summer holiday, parks are not something she enjoys.

   (B) While Mary loves the summer, holiday parks are not something she enjoys.

   _____

   _____ *1 mark*

8. **Tick ONE BOX** to show which sentence uses a **semi-colon** correctly.

   There is only one correct answer; yes. ☐

   The cat curled up in her basket; she purred contentedly. ☐

   I sat and watched Tamara; setting up her new computer. ☐

   In the hidden chamber Aladdin discovered; gold coins, rubies and diamonds. ☐

   *1 mark*

9. Complete the following sentence with an appropriate **subordinating conjunction**.

   The start of the race has been delayed _____ this sudden thunderstorm ends.

   *1 mark*

10. Circle all the **adjectives** in the following sentence.

    My   cousin's   cuddly   puppy   has   soft   fur   and   caramel   eyes.

    *1 mark*

**End of Grammar & Punctuation Test 1D ~ Now check your answers on p. 53!**

# GROUP 1 ~ Spelling Test D

1. I can never remember how to spell the word '_____'.  1 mark

2. In which _____ do you think tomatoes became popular in Europe?  1 mark

3. Parcels and letters are _____ delivered to us by mistake.  1 mark

4. "Did you catch last night's cooking _____?" inquired Steve.  1 mark

5. All I plan to do _____ is to catch up on some sleep.  1 mark

6. "Are there any tickets _____ for tonight?" she asked.  1 mark

7. I wonder how often people buy a new _____.  1 mark

8. How far can a cheetah run in a _____?  1 mark

9. "I never thought I would _____ an ogre a friend," admitted Sir Toby.  1 mark

10. Joel hoped his sore throat wasn't going to _____ into a cough.  1 mark

**End of Spelling Test 1D ~ Now check your answers!**

## GROUP 1 ~ Grammar & Punctuation Test E

1. Using a word from the same **word family** as <u>ease</u>, complete each of the following sentences.

   I'm sure you will find these exercises _____ .
   
   ↑
   
   ease

   I'm sure you will do these exercises _____ .
   
   ↑
   
   ease
   
   1 mark

2. Rewrite the sentence below in the **active**. Make sure you punctuate your answer correctly.

   The lecture will be given by Mrs Smythe.
   
   _____
   
   1 mark

3. Circle the **co-ordinating conjunction** in the following sentence.

   Although Brian was unhappy with his picture and wished he had used brighter colours, I thought his painting looked better with the darker shades.
   
   1 mark

4. Circle the **adverb** in the following sentence.

   I think my trusty old laptop needs to be rebooted; it's become very sluggish.
   
   1 mark

5. Rewrite the question below as a **statement**. You may only use the words given. Make sure you punctuate your answer correctly.

   Can Penelope juggle oranges?
   
   _____
   
   1 mark

17

**6.** **Tick ONE BOX** in each row to show if <u>after</u> is an **adverb** or a **conjunction**.

| SENTENCE | Adverb | Conjunction |
|---|---|---|
| I visited some friends in Leeds <u>after</u> Christmas was over. | | |
| A week later, <u>after</u> we had a lot of fun, I went to Bristol. | | |
| I finally got back home the week <u>after</u>. | | |

1 mark

**7.** Rewrite the sentence below in the **passive**. Make sure you punctuate your answer correctly.

Mr Garcia called Mr Jones last Thursday.

_____

1 mark

**8.** Circle all the **conjunctions** in the following sentence.

While Natasha's parents would like her to study accounting, she wants to become an archaeologist because she loves history and mythology.

1 mark

**9.** Circle the three **determiners** in the following sentence.

"Any person who doesn't drop their ball gets a prize!" yelled Farouk enthusiastically.

1 mark

**10.** Insert **capital letters** and **full stops** in the following passage so that it is punctuated correctly.

the fossils of an unknown dinosaur have been found museums around the world are very excited they are preparing lots of exhibitions to display the precious fossils

1 mark

**End of Grammar & Punctuation Test 1E ~ Now check your answers on p. 54!**

## GROUP 1 ~ Spelling Test E

1. I took part in an egg-and-spoon race and came _____.  1 mark

2. Anika is very _____ to her pet hamsters.  1 mark

3. Bored, Luiz looked around for something to _____ him.  1 mark

4. _____ winners will be selected at random from the audience.  1 mark

5. The twin sisters' _____ resemblance was quite extraordinary.  1 mark

6. With _____ grins on their faces, the goblins slunk off.  1 mark

7. "You must listen to your _____, child," the kindly queen said.  1 mark

8. Paul found an old _____ in the bushes at the end of the garden.  1 mark

9. Trekking _____ the forest, they could hear wolves howling.  1 mark

10. It took Zak a _____ of an hour to get ready.  1 mark

### End of Spelling Test 1E ~ Now check your answers!

## GROUP 2 ~ Grammar & Punctuation Test A

**1.** Form the **antonym** of each word by adding a **prefix** to it. Use a different prefix each time.

_____correct

_____regular

_____balanced

1 mark

**2.** **Tick ONE BOX** in each row to show if the underlined word is a **verb**, a **noun** or an **adjective**.

| SENTENCE | Verb | Noun | Adjective |
| --- | --- | --- | --- |
| Suleiman felt sympathy for his friend Vera. | | | |
| It was easy for him to sympathise with her. | | | |
| She had been sympathetic when he was sad. | | | |

1 mark

**3.** Insert a **colon** in the correct place in the following sentence.

That presentation was sloppy the slides were out of order and full of spelling mistakes.

1 mark

**4.** Circle the **object** of the following sentence.

Nelson stared at the large parcel on his doorstep.

1 mark

**5.** Show which **sentences** have been punctuated correctly. **Tick AS MANY BOXES** as you need to.

I can have an ice cream if I eat my greens? ☐

If I eat my greens, can I have an ice cream? ☐

Can I have an ice cream after I eat my greens? ☐

After I eat my greens, I can have an ice cream? ☐

1 mark

6. Insert a **pair of dashes** in the correct place in the following sentence.

Amit's brother was unhappy as in really unhappy to have been asked to do this.

1 mark

7. Circle the **relative pronoun** in each of the following sentences.

At the bottom of the garden was a tree that was at least two hundred years old.

It was not a tree which had shapely leaves, or interesting bark, or sweet-smelling blossom.

It was special, however, because it had been planted by a relative whose name no one could say properly.

1 mark

8. Insert a **comma** after the **fronted adverbial** in each of the following sentences.

Beneath the starry skies the explorers rode in silence.

Hopefully scientists will be able to explain this phenomenon soon.

1 mark

9. Insert one **apostrophe** in the correct place in the following sentence.

Travis always drives his mothers car to the mechanics for her.

1 mark

10. **Tick ONE BOX** to show which sentence is punctuated correctly.

"I thought the plot was rather run-of-the-mill," noted the critic. ☐

"I thought the plot was rather run-of the mill," noted the critic. ☐

"I thought the plot was rather-run-of the mill," noted the critic. ☐

"I thought the plot was rather-run-of-the-mill," noted the critic. ☐

1 mark

**End of Grammar & Punctuation Test 2A ~ Now check your answers on p. 54!**

## GROUP 2 ~ Spelling Test A

1. If he doesn't eat regularly, his _____ growls very loudly!  1 mark

2. Auntie Mabel has never found it _____ to get to sleep.  1 mark

3. Iris has travelled to a _____ of places in South America.  1 mark

4. Angie refuses to walk past the _____ after dusk.  1 mark

5. Historians do not yet know the _____ of the person in the portrait.  1 mark

6. The 'hamstring' is a _____ at the back of the thigh.  1 mark

7. "_____ is SO boring," complained the student.  1 mark

8. Kristen groaned when she saw the _____ at the box office.  1 mark

9. "I can't believe you've won _____ times in a row!" he exclaimed.  1 mark

10. "I'd _____ a hand with these suitcases!" yelled Enzo.  1 mark

### End of Spelling Test 2A ~ Now check your answers!

# GROUP 2 ~ Grammar & Punctuation Test B

1. **Tick ONE BOX** to show which sentence is a **question**.

   I wasn't listening to Paul ☐

   Did you hear what he was saying ☐

   I have no idea what to do next ☐

   Ask him to repeat his instructions ☐

   *1 mark*

2. **Tick ONE BOX** in each row to show if the sentence is a **statement** or a **question**.

   | SENTENCE | Statement | Question |
   | --- | --- | --- |
   | Why are you leaving so early | | |
   | Why he has changed jobs is a mystery | | |
   | Why do we have to go through this again | | |
   | Why the fridge wasn't working was unclear | | |

   *1 mark*

3. Draw a line to connect each word to a **suffix** to make four different words. You may use each **suffix** only once.

   | Word | | Suffix |
   | --- | --- | --- |
   | acid | | er |
   | pain | | ise |
   | modern | | ic |
   | build | | ful |

   *1 mark*

4. Insert a **comma** in the correct place in the following sentence.

   Freya lost her fluffy mittens bobble hat and stripy scarf.

   *1 mark*

5. **Tick ONE BOX** to show which pair of words are **antonyms**.

   author — co-author ☐

   port — export ☐

   habit — inhabit ☐

   possible — impossible ☐

   *1 mark*

**6.** Circle one word in each underlined pair to complete the sentences below in **Standard English**.

Using less / fewer salt in that dough would make it healthier.

"I'm glad you bought / brought this to my attention," Greta said.

Harry sailed past / passed us on his new skateboard.

1 mark

**7.** **Tick ONE BOX** to identify the sentence that shows the meeting is **least likely** to be cancelled.

Although it is snowing, the meeting mightn't be cancelled. ☐

Although it is snowing, the meeting won't be cancelled. ☐

Although it is snowing, the meeting shouldn't be cancelled. ☐

Although it is snowing, the meeting oughtn't to be cancelled. ☐

1 mark

**8.** Insert a pair of **dashes** in the correct place in the following sentence.

Ryan who has never much liked classical music has discovered he enjoys listening to Ravel.

1 mark

**9.** **Tick ONE BOX** to show which sentence is the **least formal**.

We've got to make sure we've got all our ducks in a row. ☐

We must make certain that everything is ready. ☐

It is crucial that everything be correctly organized. ☐

Please ensure that you have prepared everything. ☐

1 mark

**10.** Circle two words that are **synonyms** of each other in the following sentence.

The dazzling display of fireworks exploded in the night sky, filling it with bangs and brilliant bursts of colour.

1 mark

*End of Grammar & Punctuation Test 2B ~ Now check your answers on p. 54!*

# GROUP 2 ~ Spelling Test B

1. "I can't _____," Rafael declared. "You choose for us."   1 mark

2. These _____ events make no sense to any of us.   1 mark

3. A small _____ of farmers lived in the Arcona Valley.   1 mark

4. It is still not _____ how serious the situation is.   1 mark

5. My cousin claims I was very _____ as a child.   1 mark

6. "What does driving an electric _____ feel like?" asked Stan.   1 mark

7. The travellers hired a _____ to lead them through the canyons.   1 mark

8. In 1900, these ideas would have sparked much _____.   1 mark

9. Joe and I always argue over the _____ of the word 'either'.   1 mark

10. Tamar has an _____ memory; it is quite remarkable.   1 mark

**End of Spelling Test 2B ~ Now check your answers!**

# GROUP 2 ~ Grammar & Punctuation Test C

**1.** Using a word from the same **word family** as <u>angry</u>, complete each of the following sentences.

He shook his fist _____ at the group of naughty children.
(↑ angry)

He shook his fist in _____ at the group of naughty children.    1 mark
(↑ angry)

**2.** Rewrite the sentence below in the **passive**. Make sure you punctuate your answer correctly.

The mouse has eaten all the peanuts.

_____    1 mark

**3.** Circle the **subordinating conjunction** in the following sentence.

I find it comforting when the birds chirp in the morning; it reminds me of being a child and living in the countryside.    1 mark

**4.** Circle the **adjective** in the following sentence.

We gaped in amazement at the kaleidoscopic colours created by the gemstones.    1 mark

**5.** Rewrite the statement below as a **question**. You may only use the words given. Make sure you punctuate your answer correctly.

The Thompson twins were really rude.

_____    1 mark

26

6. **Tick ONE BOX** in each row to show if <u>since</u> is a **preposition** or a **conjunction**.

| SENTENCE | Preposition | Conjunction |
|---|---|---|
| Helena has not been on a holiday <u>since</u> 2019. | | |
| This is not good for her <u>since</u> her job is tiring. | | |
| In fact, she has been given more work <u>since</u> her boss left. | | |

1 mark

7. Rewrite the sentence below in the **active**. Make sure you punctuate your answer correctly.

   The Rosetta Stone was discovered by French soldiers.

   _____
   
   1 mark

8. Circle all the **conjunctions** in the following sentence.

   In the winter, I try to go walking and jogging in our local park every week although I hate the cold.
   
   1 mark

9. Circle the three **determiners** in the following sentence.

   Each and every day, Priscilla trudged to the village well to fetch fresh water.
   
   1 mark

10. Insert **capital letters** and **full stops** in the following passage so that it is punctuated correctly.

    there was only a short time to go in a few minutes, the space shuttle would take off and begin its journey the astronauts could not believe it was finally happening
    
    1 mark

........ **End of Grammar & Punctuation Test 2C ~ Now check your answers on p. 54!** ........

## GROUP 2 ~ Spelling Test C

1. I'm not sure I would _____ Kevin if I saw him now.  1 mark

2. Prince Ali was _____ to be found sitting by the magic fountain.  1 mark

3. The _____ temples were exceptionally magnificent at sunset.  1 mark

4. Extreme weather events can have _____ impacts on cities.  1 mark

5. "Is all that shrieking really _____?" Sophia asked irritably.  1 mark

6. Overnight, the large _____ sailed out towards the ocean.  1 mark

7. Vijay insisted that he didn't have a _____ song.  1 mark

8. "Are you _____ that is the right answer?" Gerald asked.  1 mark

9. It did not _____ to Yonas to check the website.  1 mark

10. Those manufacturers _____ their products for ten years.  1 mark

**End of Spelling Test 2C ~ Now check your answers!**

## GROUP 2 ~ Grammar & Punctuation Test D

1. **Tick ONE BOX** to show which sentence is punctuated correctly.

   That recycling bin which is used for paper and cardboard, has been full for days. ☐

   That recycling bin, which is used for paper and cardboard has been full for days. ☐

   That recycling bin, which is used for paper and cardboard, has been full for days. ☐

   That recycling bin which, is used for paper and cardboard, has been full for days. ☐

   *1 mark*

2. Insert a **semi-colon** in the correct place in the following sentence.

   The coffee machine is making strange sounds it shouldn't be used for now.

   *1 mark*

3. **Tick ONE BOX** to show which sentence uses the word <u>smell</u> as a **noun**.

   "Ew! What's that awful <u>smell</u>?" squealed Pippa. ☐

   "I'm sorry my hands <u>smell</u> of onions. I've been cooking," Sean said. ☐

   "Can you <u>smell</u> the jasmine on that side of the garden?" called Gina. ☐

   "I believe," said Ira, "that I <u>smell</u> a rat." ☐

   *1 mark*

4. Rewrite the verbs that are underlined below so that they are in the **simple present**.

   Maria regularly <u>gave</u> me a lift to work as we <u>were</u> neighbours.

   [ ]     [ ]

   *1 mark*

5. **Tick ONE BOX** to show which sentence is the **least formal**.

   Jared and I had our eyes firmly fixed on the television. ☐

   Jared and I gazed constantly at the TV. ☐

   Jared and I could not stop staring at the telly. ☐

   Jared and I were glued to the box. ☐

   *1 mark*

29

6. Insert **inverted commas** in the correct place in the following sentence.

   Is that an antique table ? inquired Mel .

   1 mark

7. **Tick ONE BOX** to show which option completes the sentence using the **past progressive**.

   A herd of bison _____ across the plain.

   thundered ☐

   had thundered ☐

   were thundering ☐

   will thunder ☐

   1 mark

8. **Tick ONE BOX** in each row to show if the apostrophe is used for **possession** or **contraction**.

   | SENTENCE | Possession | Contraction |
   |---|---|---|
   | I think the film's ending was a bit silly. | | |
   | Jessie is sorry that she can't come. | | |
   | It'll take us hours to sort this mess out. | | |

   1 mark

9. Replace the underlined word or words in the passage below with the correct **pronouns**.

   As the weather was warm, Maria decided to go swimming. The weather

   [        ]

   suddenly turned cold, so Maria changed her mind.

   [        ]

   1 mark

10. **Tick ONE BOX** to show which sentence uses **tense** correctly.

    Lucy had travelled a lot and visits many countries. ☐

    Just as she suspected, her friends had organised a party for her. ☐

    As he promises, Tim has fed my aunt's fish. ☐

    They are volunteering for many charities and made an impact. ☐

    1 mark

**End of Grammar & Punctuation Test 2D ~ Now check your answers on p. 55!**

## GROUP 2 ~ Spelling Test D

1. Dan claims to speak six _____ languages fluently.    1 mark

2. "Why do you _____ everything?" she asked impatiently.    1 mark

3. Annoyingly, his cousin always seems to _____ with our plans.    1 mark

4. Carla's younger brother solemnly promised not to be a _____.    1 mark

5. "Is 10 o'clock a _____ time for you?" Faisal asked.    1 mark

6. Our local _____ dramatics club puts on several plays a year.    1 mark

7. "Do you _____ where I agreed to meet Sue?" Tina asked me.    1 mark

8. While picturesque, the old narrow roads were a _____ to traffic.    1 mark

9. "I wouldn't _____ the pumpkin soup," whispered the waiter.    1 mark

10. "Arrgh! I've just deleted my files by _____," groaned Gita.    1 mark

**End of Spelling Test 2D ~ Now check your answers!**

# GROUP 2 ~ Grammar & Punctuation Test E

1. Show what the **question mark** could tell you about the following sentence. **Tick AS MANY BOXES** as you need to.

   "Who has borrowed my umbrella?"

   It shows that there is something that the person does not know. ☐

   It shows that the person is whispering. ☐

   It shows that the person would like someone else to say something. ☐

   It shows that the person has not finished talking. ☐

   *1 mark*

2. Circle the **possessive pronoun** in the following sentence.

   "That's my hot dog, not yours! Don't you dare take it!" he growled.

   *1 mark*

3. Using the boxes given, write the **expanded forms** of the underlined words.

   I think that Olivia and Marco could've been delayed by traffic, but I think

   [ ]

   they'd have called to let us know.

   [ ]

   *1 mark*

4. Underline the **relative clause** in the following sentence.

   The ageing actor whose performance made me cry has won an Oscar.

   *1 mark*

5. **Tick ONE BOX** to show what the underlined words in the sentence below are called.

   <u>That grand, red-brick building</u>, which was constructed in 1845, is now a photography gallery.

   a noun phrase ☐

   a fronted adverbial ☐

   a relative clause ☐

   a main clause ☐

   *1 mark*

**6.** **Tick TWO BOXES** to show which sentences contain a **preposition**.

| | |
|---|---|
| Shereen checked the hutch by the shed. | ☐ |
| She had lost her pet rabbit. | ☐ |
| He was called "Mr Muffin" and had white fur. | ☐ |
| She hadn't seen him since breakfast. | ☐ |
| No one else had seen him either. | ☐ |

1 mark

**7.** How does the position of the **comma** change the meanings of the following sentences?

(A) While Pete stared at the dinosaur model, fossils were being shown to the children.

(B) While Pete stared at the dinosaur, model fossils were being shown to the children.

_____

_____

1 mark

**8.** **Tick ONE BOX** to show which sentence uses a **semi-colon** correctly.

| | |
|---|---|
| Of her qualities, one was the most popular; honesty. | ☐ |
| We loved; sampling the fruit, homemade jams and fresh bread at the market. | ☐ |
| They run their own business; the hours are long, but it is rewarding. | ☐ |
| The poem ended with the friendly dolphin; swimming out to sea. | ☐ |

1 mark

**9.** Complete the following sentence with an appropriate **co-ordinating conjunction**.

The movie we were watching was unusually long, _____ we were all gripped to the very end.

1 mark

**10.** Circle all the **adjectives** in the following sentence.

My   boots   are   sturdy   and   reliable;   I   don't   care   that   they   are   plain.

1 mark

**End of Grammar & Punctuation Test 2E ~ Now check your answers on p. 55!**

# GROUP 2 ~ Spelling Test E

1. "Is this going to be a formal _____?" Siobhan asked.  1 mark

2. Years ago, people wrote letters to _____ with each other.  1 mark

3. I was unconvinced by her _____ of events.  1 mark

4. She noticed a curious _____ on the old silver coin.  1 mark

5. Justine was _____ nice to me today; I've no idea why.  1 mark

6. "I'm NEVER going back to that _____!" fumed Mario.  1 mark

7. Alma has been given the thrilling _____ to work on a film set.  1 mark

8. He is scared of dogs; it doesn't matter if they are _____ or not.  1 mark

9. The High Priestess was famous for her _____ of medicine.  1 mark

10. I still find the _____ "Thirty days hath September..." useful.  1 mark

## End of Spelling Test 2E ~ Now check your answers!

# GROUP 3 ~ Grammar & Punctuation Test A

1. Using a word from the same **word family** as <u>sad</u>, complete each of the following sentences.

   "Most of the magical creatures have left," said the fairy _____.
   ↑
   [sad]

   "Most of the magical creatures have left," said the fairy with _____.  1 mark
   ↑
   [sad]

2. Rewrite the sentence below in the **active**. Make sure you punctuate your answer correctly.

   The mystery was solved by Sherlock Holmes.

   _____  1 mark

3. Circle the **co-ordinating conjunction** in the following sentence.

   Although he loves food with strong flavours, Pierre doesn't eat anything that is described as 'spicy', for he is allergic to chillies.  1 mark

4. Circle the **determiner** in the following sentence.

   I think you will find some old woollen socks in Harvey's messy bottom drawer.  1 mark

5. Rewrite the question below as a **statement**. You may only use the words given. Make sure you punctuate your answer correctly.

   Has the programme started already?

   _____  1 mark

35

**6.** Tick **ONE BOX** in each row to show if <u>before</u> is a **preposition** or a **conjunction**.

| SENTENCE | Preposition | Conjunction |
|---|---|---|
| Fabiana stood <u>before</u> the large library doors. | | |
| <u>Before</u> she could go in, she needed a ticket. | | |
| A lot of people were in the queue <u>before</u> her. | | |

1 mark

**7.** Rewrite the sentence below in the **active**. Make sure you punctuate your answer correctly.

Every year, the Festival of the Sun was held by the Incas.

_____

1 mark

**8.** Circle all the **conjunctions** in the following sentence.

On Midsummer's Eve, when the woodland elves come out to celebrate, there is always much feasting and merriment since they love parties.

1 mark

**9.** Circle the three **determiners** in the following sentence.

Have we got enough seats? There are two chairs in here and three stools outside.

1 mark

**10.** Insert **capital letters** and **full stops** in the following passage so that it is punctuated correctly.

deep beneath the waves, the wreck lay on the ocean floor it had been there in silence and in darkness for almost two hundred years all that, however, was about to change

1 mark

*End of Grammar & Punctuation Test 3A ~ Now check your answers on p. 55!*

36

## GROUP 3 ~ Spelling Test A

1. Please include your email _____ on the form.    1 mark

2. You can decorate your room _____ you like.    1 mark

3. "I will help _____ you with survival skills," said the instructor.    1 mark

4. "I have long wondered about the _____ of ghosts," he confessed.    1 mark

5. A real-life example of _____ lines are the rungs of a ladder.    1 mark

6. "He never has anything _____ to say," she grumbled.    1 mark

7. Frankie narrowly avoided a _____ with a cyclist.    1 mark

8. For some odd reason, _____ is Ida's favourite day of the week.    1 mark

9. "I can't _____ through my blocked nose," complained Willow.    1 mark

10. The woodland elves made many a _____ to help save the fairies.    1 mark

**End of Spelling Test 3A ~ Now check your answers!**

## GROUP 3 ~ Grammar & Punctuation Test B

**1.** Form the **antonym** of each word by adding a **prefix** to it. Use a different prefix each time.

_____practical

_____complete

_____please

1 mark

**2.** Tick ONE BOX in each row to show if the underlined word is a **verb**, a **noun** or an **adjective**.

| SENTENCE | Verb | Noun | Adjective |
|---|---|---|---|
| Dictionaries list words in <u>alphabetical</u> order. | | | |
| There are 26 letters in the English <u>alphabet</u>. | | | |
| It would take days to <u>alphabetise</u> the books in our library. | | | |

1 mark

**3.** Insert a **colon** in the correct place in the following sentence.

Our local playground was very popular it had loads of swings, slides, sandboxes and climbing frames.

1 mark

**4.** Circle the **subject** of the following sentence.

Jacques studied history at the Sorbonne in Paris.

1 mark

**5.** Show which **sentences** have been punctuated correctly. **Tick AS MANY BOXES** as you need to.

Rosa can see her friends if she finishes her homework? ☐

Can Rosa see her friends once she finishes her homework? ☐

Once Rosa finishes her homework, she can see her friends? ☐

If Rosa finishes her homework, can she see her friends? ☐

1 mark

38

**6.** Insert a **pair of dashes** in the correct place in the following sentence.

She was overjoyed positively ecstatic when she was told she'd not broken her ankle.

*1 mark*

**7.** Circle the **relative pronoun** in each of the following sentences.

Fran, whose phone rang in the middle of the film, was rather embarrassed.

She didn't like being the person who had forgotten to mute her mobile.

She was also annoyed because she did not know the number that had rung her.

*1 mark*

**8.** Insert a **comma** after the **fronted adverbial** in each of the following sentences.

Immediately after the loud boom all the passengers rushed to the ship's deck.

According to local legend the nearby forest is haunted by a knight.

*1 mark*

**9.** Insert one **apostrophe** in the correct place in the following sentence.

Usually, Iris removes a hardbacks dust cover before she reads it.

*1 mark*

**10. Tick ONE BOX** to show which sentence is punctuated correctly.

Juanita has had a-state-of-the-art laser printer set up in her office. ☐

Juanita has had a state-of-the-art-laser printer set up in her office. ☐

Juanita has had a state-of-the art laser printer set up in her office. ☐

Juanita has had a state-of-the-art laser printer set up in her office. ☐

*1 mark*

······( **End of Grammar & Punctuation Test 3B ~ Now check your answers on p. 55!** )······

## GROUP 3 ~ Spelling Test B

1. My baby brother says 'soldier' for '_____'.  1 mark

2. Once the work is done, I'll send it to Eric _____.  1 mark

3. At the crossroads, the two wizards went their _____ ways.  1 mark

4. "I have, _____, decided to resign," finished the mayor.  1 mark

5. Zane has just taken part in his first science _____.  1 mark

6. "Have you considered a career in local _____?" he asked her.  1 mark

7. "Is there a _____ monument you want to see?" Murphy asked.  1 mark

8. "I've just made a _____ discovery!" said Una excitedly.  1 mark

9. "There is much I wish to _____," the young inventor declared.  1 mark

10. They watched the sun gradually _____ behind the mountains.  1 mark

**End of Spelling Test 3B ~ Now check your answers!**

## GROUP 3 ~ Grammar & Punctuation Test C

1. **Tick ONE BOX** to show which sentence is punctuated correctly.

   Our new kitten whose, name is Cuddles, is chasing butterflies in the garden. ☐

   Our new kitten, whose name is Cuddles, is chasing butterflies in the garden. ☐

   Our new kitten, whose name is Cuddles is chasing butterflies in the garden. ☐

   Our new kitten whose name is Cuddles, is chasing butterflies in the garden. ☐

   1 mark

2. Insert a **dash** in the correct place in the following sentence.

   Matt has just flown to South Africa he's wanted to go there all his life!

   1 mark

3. **Tick ONE BOX** to show which sentence uses the word <u>back</u> as an **adjective**.

   I've decided I'm going to <u>back</u> Manchester City this season. ☐

   "There is something wrong with my <u>back</u>; it really hurts," said Ivan. ☐

   I'm sure there was a fox in our <u>back</u> garden last night. ☐

   Rachel noticed something odd on the <u>back</u> of the envelope. ☐

   1 mark

4. Rewrite the verbs that are underlined below so that they are in the **simple past**.

   Mrs Simpson always <u>leaves</u> a night light on when Tommy <u>goes</u> to bed.

   [    ]          [    ]

   1 mark

5. **Tick ONE BOX** to show which sentence is the **least informal**.

   Trish was unable to make sense of his conduct. ☐

   Trish could not get her head around his actions. ☐

   Trish didn't understand his behaviour. ☐

   Trish was at a loss to figure out what he'd done. ☐

   1 mark

**6.** Insert **inverted commas** in the correct place in the following sentence.

Did that dog bark at you ? asked Sylvia .

1 mark

**7.** Tick **ONE BOX** to show which option completes the sentence using the **simple present**.

I don't know how actors _____ their lines every night.

are going to remember ☐

remember ☐

have been remembering ☐

had remembered ☐

1 mark

**8.** Tick **ONE BOX** in each row to show if the apostrophe is used for **possession** or **contraction**.

| SENTENCE | Possession | Contraction |
|---|---|---|
| Where's the remote disappeared to now? | | |
| If you've got time, please help. | | |
| Arvind tried to find the children's skittles. | | |

1 mark

**9.** Replace the underlined word or words in the passage below with the correct **pronouns**.

Both the novel and the film have been hugely successful. <u>The novel and the film</u>

[ ]

have made loads of money; <u>the novel and the film</u> have also won many awards.

[ ]

1 mark

**10.** Tick **ONE BOX** to show which sentence uses **tense** correctly.

Rita mops the floor before Samir was cleaning the mirrors. ☐

While Raja was exploring the forest, he spots a rare shrub. ☐

We were waiting for Helena when our phones rang. ☐

A dramatic storm is beginning as Liam and Ida drove home. ☐

1 mark

*End of Grammar & Punctuation Test 3C ~ Now check your answers on p. 56!*

42

# GROUP 3 ~ Spelling Test C

1. Did you know that a group of owls is called a '_____ of owls'?  1 mark

2. "There's a _____ smell coming from the fridge," sniffed Lily.  1 mark

3. Ben and Jerry have had an _____ over whose turn it is.  1 mark

4. The manager's _____ was unbelievably rude to me.  1 mark

5. "I haven't come to _____; I've come to help," she said.  1 mark

6. If you are concerned, _____ you should call Maggie.  1 mark

7. Ivan couldn't _____ a single good film to watch.  1 mark

8. "The _____ who made this mess must clean it up," he said.  1 mark

9. Aida's sense of _____ makes her an ideal drummer.  1 mark

10. "Your _____ is just as illegible as mine!" huffed Suzanne.  1 mark

**End of Spelling Test 3C ~ Now check your answers!**

# GROUP 3 ~ Grammar & Punctuation Test D

1. Show what the **comma** could tell you about the following sentence. **Tick AS MANY BOXES** as you need to.

    "There's no salad left in the fridge,"

    It shows that the person does not like eating salad. ☐

    It shows that the person is making a statement. ☐

    It shows that the person is not shouting. ☐

    It shows that the person is asking a question. ☐

    *1 mark*

2. Circle the **possessive pronoun** in the following sentence.

    I had to borrow my neighbour's lawnmower since mine was being repaired. *1 mark*

3. Using the boxes given, write the **contracted forms** of the underlined words.

    We certainly <u>have not</u> forgotten about Emma's surprise party;

    ☐

    <u>we will</u> definitely be there on Friday evening!

    ☐

    *1 mark*

4. Underline the **relative clause** in the following sentence.

    My uncle who sells curious antiques always has interesting stories to tell us. *1 mark*

5. **Tick ONE BOX** to show what the underlined words in the sentence below are called.

    <u>That restaurant is regularly full of customers</u>, so it's generally very noisy.

    a subordinate clause ☐

    a main clause ☐

    a noun phrase ☐

    a relative clause ☐

    *1 mark*

6. **Tick TWO BOXES** to show which sentences contain a **preposition**.

   Last Saturday evening, Tuber the Troll was grumpy. ☐

   So, he went and sat underneath a bridge. ☐

   He soon realised he could hear a voice. ☐

   "Help! You're hurting me!" squeaked the voice. ☐

   Tuber looked, but he couldn't see anyone near him. ☐

   1 mark

7. How does the position of the **comma** change the meanings of the following sentences?

   (A) As Fiona admired the cave art, books were being sold to tourists.

   (B) As Fiona admired the cave, art books were being sold to tourists.

   _____

   _____

   1 mark

8. **Tick ONE BOX** to show which sentence uses a **semi-colon** correctly.

   Veronika's stew was delicious; her guests had to have second helpings. ☐

   They could not decide; if they wanted the puzzles, the Lego, or the board games. ☐

   Ahmed has been taking lessons; learning a second language. ☐

   The travellers decided to head for the capital; Bangkok. ☐

   1 mark

9. Complete the following sentence with an appropriate **subordinating conjunction**.

   "_____ you wish to remain my captive, you must do as I command," ordered the wizard.

   1 mark

10. Circle all the **adjectives** in the following sentence.

    Rob was startled by the sudden, screeching sound.

    1 mark

**End of Grammar & Punctuation Test 3D ~ Now check your answers on p. 56!**

## GROUP 3 ~ Spelling Test D

1. Lydia found a _____ of rope at the bottom of the chest.  1 mark

2. "_____ to local legend," said Yuki, "that cottage is haunted."  1 mark

3. We believe we have _____ local support for our plans.  1 mark

4. Unlike Khaled, I can't concentrate in a noisy _____.  1 mark

5. For the dwarves, the day had started like any other _____ day.  1 mark

6. Mrs Maher found it easy to _____ Kelly to join her for lunch.  1 mark

7. "Ooh! That's a nasty _____! What happened?" asked Anton.  1 mark

8. "Do you think his apology was _____?" she wondered.  1 mark

9. Much of Omar's _____ time is spent taking photographs.  1 mark

10. What do you call a word that has the _____ meaning to another?  1 mark

**End of Spelling Test 3D ~ Now check your answers!**

## GROUP 3 ~ Grammar & Punctuation Test E

1. **Tick ONE BOX** to show which sentence is an **exclamation**.

   What a brilliant person that scientist is ☐

   She has unlocked the mystery of dark energy ☐

   Her findings have been published globally ☐

   She'll definitely win lots of prizes, won't she ☐

   *1 mark*

2. **Tick ONE BOX** in each row to show if the sentence is a **statement** or a **question**.

   | SENTENCE | Statement | Question |
   |---|---|---|
   | Where are the next Winter Olympics going to be held | | |
   | Where the bandits vanished to is unknown | | |
   | Where all this will end is anyone's guess | | |
   | Where has Diana put my muddy boots | | |

   *1 mark*

3. Draw a line to connect each word to a **suffix** to make four different words. You may use each **suffix** only once.

   | Word | Suffix |
   |---|---|
   | edit | age |
   | access | ify |
   | pack | ible |
   | just | or |

   *1 mark*

4. Insert a **comma** in the correct place in the following sentence.

   The burglar climbed over the wall crept up the path and hid in the shadows.

   *1 mark*

5. **Tick ONE BOX** to show which pair of words are **antonyms**.

   visit     revisit ☐

   operate     cooperate ☐

   behave     misbehave ☐

   star     superstar ☐

   *1 mark*

47

**6.** Circle one word in each underlined pair to complete the sentences below in **Standard English**.

"Your fish is bigger then / **than** mine," Ed grumbled.

The evidence lead / **led** the detective to an abandoned farm.

After 6 o'clock, there is usually **no one** / noone left in the office.

1 mark

**7.** **Tick ONE BOX** to identify the sentence that shows Olga is **most unlikely** to visit her cousins.

Next week, Olga shall be visiting her cousins in Carlisle. ☐

Next week, Olga will be visiting her cousins in Carlisle. ☐

Next week, Olga might be visiting her cousins in Carlisle. ☐

Next week, Olga should be visiting her cousins in Carlisle. ☐

1 mark

**8.** Insert a pair of **commas** in the correct place in the following sentence.

Felicia, who normally avoids rich desserts, enjoyed the double-chocolate brownies.

1 mark

**9.** **Tick ONE BOX** to show which sentence is the **least informal**.

I really think Danny should come clean about everything. ☐

In my opinion, Danny should be truthful about the events. ☐

I feel that Danny needs to tell us what really happened. ☐

I believe it essential that Danny tell the truth about the events. ☐

1 mark

**10.** Circle two words that are **synonyms** of each other in the following sentence.

Exasperated by Caleb's repeated interruptions, Wendy snapped at him in an irritated tone.

1 mark

**End of Grammar & Punctuation Test 3E ~ Now check your answers on p. 56!**

# GROUP 3 ~ Spelling Test E

1. A synonym for the word '_____' is 'intolerance'.  1 mark

2. Our team's _____ score was much higher than we expected.  1 mark

3. Last Saturday, our _____ was visited by several loud guests.  1 mark

4. "Don't nag!" snapped Ira. "I am _____ of the time!"  1 mark

5. Our stadium can _____ up to 60,000 spectators.  1 mark

6. Uncle Gavin claims that chicken soup is the secret of his _____.  1 mark

7. Yolanda frequently makes comments that aren't _____.  1 mark

8. "I'm sorry! I didn't mean to _____ you!" exclaimed Seth.  1 mark

9. Fran always lets her _____ get the better of her.  1 mark

10. "That is _____ and utter nonsense," scoffed Jason.  1 mark

**End of Spelling Test 3E ~ Now check your answers!**

# Student Progress Chart

As you work through the tests in this book, why not keep a record of how you are doing?
Don't worry if you don't get *all* of the answers right first time around.
Making mistakes is one important way we learn new things.
Good luck!

| GROUP 1 | #1 | #2 | #3 | #4 | #5 | #6 | #7 | #8 | #9 | #10 | TOTAL | DATE |
|---|---|---|---|---|---|---|---|---|---|---|---|---|
| Grammar & Punctuation Test 1.A | | | | | | | | | | | | |
| Spelling Test 1.A | | | | | | | | | | | | |
| Grammar & Punctuation Test 1.B | | | | | | | | | | | | |
| Spelling Test 1.B | | | | | | | | | | | | |
| Grammar & Punctuation Test 1.C | | | | | | | | | | | | |
| Spelling Test 1.C | | | | | | | | | | | | |
| Grammar & Punctuation Test 1.D | | | | | | | | | | | | |
| Spelling Test 1.D | | | | | | | | | | | | |
| Grammar & Punctuation Test 1.E | | | | | | | | | | | | |
| Spelling Test 1.E | | | | | | | | | | | | |

| GROUP 2 | #1 | #2 | #3 | #4 | #5 | #6 | #7 | #8 | #9 | #10 | TOTAL | DATE |
|---|---|---|---|---|---|---|---|---|---|---|---|---|
| Grammar & Punctuation Test 2.A | | | | | | | | | | | | |
| Spelling Test 2.A | | | | | | | | | | | | |
| Grammar & Punctuation Test 2.B | | | | | | | | | | | | |
| Spelling Test 2.B | | | | | | | | | | | | |
| Grammar & Punctuation Test 2.C | | | | | | | | | | | | |
| Spelling Test 2.C | | | | | | | | | | | | |
| Grammar & Punctuation Test 2.D | | | | | | | | | | | | |
| Spelling Test 2.D | | | | | | | | | | | | |
| Grammar & Punctuation Test 2.E | | | | | | | | | | | | |
| Spelling Test 2.E | | | | | | | | | | | | |

| GROUP 3 | #1 | #2 | #3 | #4 | #5 | #6 | #7 | #8 | #9 | #10 | TOTAL | DATE |
|---|---|---|---|---|---|---|---|---|---|---|---|---|
| Grammar & Punctuation Test 3.A | | | | | | | | | | | | |
| Spelling Test 3.A | | | | | | | | | | | | |
| Grammar & Punctuation Test 3.B | | | | | | | | | | | | |
| Spelling Test 3.B | | | | | | | | | | | | |
| Grammar & Punctuation Test 3.C | | | | | | | | | | | | |
| Spelling Test 3.C | | | | | | | | | | | | |
| Grammar & Punctuation Test 3.D | | | | | | | | | | | | |
| Spelling Test 3.D | | | | | | | | | | | | |
| Grammar & Punctuation Test 3.E | | | | | | | | | | | | |
| Spelling Test 3.E | | | | | | | | | | | | |

# Grammar & Punctuation Tests
- Administration & Marking Guidelines
- Answers

# Spelling Tests
- Administration & Marking Guidelines
- Transcripts

# Grammar & Punctuation Tests: Administration & Marking Guidelines

## Using the Grammar & Punctuation Tests

All the tests in this book have been designed for you to be able to use them as one, or both, of the following:
- **Quick practice sessions** throughout the school year
- **Tools for targeted exam preparation** during revision sessions before mocks or the actual exams

Depending on how you wish to use the Grammar & Punctuation tests in this book, you may want to consider the following with regards to timing and how you award marks.

## Timing the Grammar & Punctuation Tests

If your students are actively revising for the KS2 SATs, we recommend that students **try to complete each test within 10 minutes.**

However, **it is up to you to decide** how much time to give your students.

Indeed, you may wish to remove the time factor completely so that they feel less anxious or pressured. Alternatively, you may want to make the tests a bit of a challenge. If so, set a time limit that you feel is appropriate for your students.

## Grammar & Punctuation Tests Marking Guidelines

The guidelines given below are to be followed if you want to stick to the strict government marking scheme of the actual 2023 SATs English Paper 1 exam.

**MARKS**
- In all the Grammar & Punctuation Tests, each **correctly answered question** is worth **1 mark**.
- Half marks **may not be awarded**.

**MULTIPLE ANSWERS**
- When a question **requires more than one answer**, **ALL** the student's given **responses must be correct** for their answer to be regarded as right. For example, if the correct answers are the words *happy* and *sad*, the student must provide both correct words.

On the other hand, if you would like a more flexible approach to marking, then you may wish to consider awarding half marks and/or accepting partially correct answers. Again, this is left to your discretion.

## Notes to the Answers

**MULTIPLE ANSWERS**
- When a question has **up to three possible correct answers**, all possible correct answers are listed and are separated by **OR**.
- When a question can be **correctly answered in lots of ways**, this is noted in this section and an **example** of at least **one possible correct** answer is given.

**ANSWERS TO 'TICK BOX' QUESTIONS**
- Where the student must show their chosen answer by ticking at least one box in a set of vertical boxes, this section gives the correct answer(s), followed by which box(es) should be ticked: *1st box, 2nd box, 3rd box, etc.* where **1st box corresponds to the topmost box** and so on.

# Grammar & Punctuation Tests Answers

## Grammar & Punctuation Test 1A (pp. 5-6)

**(1)** Make sure you bring your library card with you. *(4th box)*
**(2)** What a fabulous... → exclamation;
What an unsatisfying... → exclamation;
What has happened... → question;
What song were... → question
**(3)** fright → ful; laugh → ing; king → dom; dark → ness
**(4)** ...dusting <u>shelves, polishing</u> the silver...
**(5)** natural    unnatural *(2nd box)*
**(6)** (much)/ many ; (loose)/ lose ; to /(too)
**(7)** Maria will be delighted with her present. *(4th box)*
**(8)** Becca (<u>whose</u> favourite colour is <u>purple</u>) has...
**(9)** It was critical that Neil depart and travel to Chicago that day. *(3rd box)*
**(10)** deceive = betray **OR** to deceive = to betray

## Grammar & Punctuation Test 1B (pp. 8-9)

**(1)** Professor Schmidt, who is the brains behind the discovery, is quite talkative. *(1st box)*
**(2)** ...very <u>inconsiderate: they</u> constantly...
**(3)** I can't <u>face</u> another bowl of soup for supper. *(4th box)*
**(4)** makes → made; sends → sent
**(5)** Hal purchased a club sandwich since he was famished. *(2nd box)*
**(6)** "Have...shoes<u>?</u>" **OR** 'Have...shoes<u>?</u>'
**(7)** is checking *(1st box)*
**(8)** We're looking... → contraction;
The pirates'... → possession;
My classmate's... → possession
**(9)** Fred → he; Lisa and Fred → they
**(10)** Jill is happy that all her friends have managed to come. *(4th box)*

## Grammar & Punctuation Test 1C (pp. 11-12)

**(1)** <u>dis</u>continue; <u>il</u>legal; <u>mis</u>behave
**(2)** dramatize → verb; drama → noun; dramatic → adjective
**(3)** ...is <u>useless — its</u> screen...
**(4)** Alicia
**(5)** Can Ted watch TV when he has taken out the rubbish? *(1st box)*; If Ted takes out the rubbish, can he watch TV? *(4th box)*
**(6)** ...beyond <u>furious — I'm</u> not <u>exaggerating —</u> <u>about</u> his...
**(7)** Sir Percy, <u>who</u> was...;
...yelling, <u>which</u> he...;
...friend, <u>whom</u> we've...
**(8)** Irritatingly for Harry and <u>I,</u> we missed...;
Soon after <u>lunch,</u> the...
**(9)** ...many tombs<u>'</u> walls.
**(10)** Lucy delivered the astounding news in her usual matter-of-fact way. *(3rd box)*

## Grammar & Punctuation Test 1D (pp. 14-15)

**(1)** It shows that the person is not speaking quietly. *(2nd box)*; It shows that the person has definite feelings about the surprise. *(4th box)*
**(2)** ours
**(3)** must not → mustn't; it is → it's
**(4)** <u>which hangs in the hall</u>
**(5)** a subordinate clause *(1st box)*
**(6)** There were luggage racks above us. *(3rd box)*; They were full of other people's bags. *(5th box)*
**(7)** *Answers will differ, but any correct response must show an understanding that the items in (A) are 'summer holiday' & 'parks', and that the items in (B) are 'summer' & 'holiday parks'. Example: (A) shows Mary dislikes parks while (B) shows Mary dislikes holiday parks.*
**(8)** The cat curled up in her basket; she purred contentedly. *(2nd box)*
**(9)** until
**(10)** cuddly; soft; caramel

### Grammar & Punctuation Test 1E (pp. 17-18)

(1) ...find these exercises <u>easy</u>;
...do these exercises <u>easily</u>.
(2) Mrs Smythe will give the lecture. **OR** Mrs Smythe will be giving the lecture.
(3) and
(4) very
(5) Penelope can juggle oranges.
(6) ...<u>after</u> Christmas was... → conjunction;
...<u>after</u> we had... → conjunction;
the week <u>after</u>. → adverb
(7) *Answers will differ. Example:* Mr Jones was called last Thursday.
(8) While; because; and
(9) Any; their; a
(10) <u>T</u>he fossils...been foun<u>d</u>. <u>M</u>useums around...very excite<u>d</u>. <u>T</u>hey are...precious fossil<u>s</u>.

### Grammar & Punctuation Test 2A (pp. 20-21)

(1) <u>in</u>correct; <u>ir</u>regular; <u>un</u>balanced
(2) sympathy → noun; sympathise → verb; sympathetic → adjective
(3) ...was <u>sloppy: the</u> slides were...
(4) parcel **OR** large parcel **OR** the large parcel
(5) If I eat my greens, can I have an ice cream? *(2nd box)*; Can I have an ice cream after I eat my greens? *(3rd box)*
(6) ...was <u>unhappy — as</u> in really <u>unhappy — to</u> have...
(7) ...a tree <u>that</u> was...;
...a tree <u>which</u> had...;
...a relative <u>whose</u> name...
(8) Beneath the starry <u>skies,</u> the explorers...;
<u>Hopefully,</u> scientists will...
(9) ...his mother<u>'s</u> car...
(10) "I thought the plot was rather run-of-the-mill," noted the critic. *(1st box)*

### Grammar & Punctuation Test 2B (pp. 23-24)

(1) Did you hear what he was saying *(2nd box)*
(2) Why are you... → question;
Why he has... → statement;
Why do we... → question;
Why the fridge... → statement
(3) acid → ic; pain → ful; modern → ise; build → er
(4) ...fluffy <u>mittens, bobble</u> hat and...
(5) possible    impossible *(4th box)*
(6) (less)/ fewer ; bought /(brought); (past)/ passed
(7) Although it is snowing, the meeting won't be cancelled. *(2nd box)*
(8) <u>Ryan — who</u> has never much liked classical <u>music — has</u> discovered...
(9) We've got to make sure we've got all our ducks in a row. *(1st box)*
(10) dazzling = brilliant

### Grammar & Punctuation Test 2C (pp. 26-27)

(1) ...shook his fist <u>angrily</u>...;
...shook his fist in <u>anger</u>...
(2) All the peanuts have been eaten by the mouse. **OR** All the peanuts have been eaten.
(3) when
(4) kaleidoscopic
(5) Were the Thompson twins really rude?
(6) ...holiday <u>since</u> 2019. → preposition;
...<u>since</u> her job is... → conjunction;
...<u>since</u> her boss left. → conjunction
(7) French soldiers discovered the Rosetta Stone.
(8) and; although
(9) Each; every; the
(10) <u>T</u>here was...to g<u>o</u>. <u>I</u>n a few...its journe<u>y</u>. <u>T</u>he astronauts...finally happenin<u>g</u>.

### Grammar & Punctuation Test 2D (pp. 29-30)

**(1)** That recycling bin, which is used for paper and cardboard, has been full for days. *(3rd box)*
**(2)** ...strange sounds; it shouldn't...
**(3)** "Ew! What's that awful smell?" squealed Pippa. *(1st box)*
**(4)** gave → gives; were → are
**(5)** Jared and I were glued to the box. *(4th box)*
**(6)** "Is...table?" **OR** 'Is...table?'
**(7)** were thundering *(3rd box)*
**(8)** ...the film's... → possession;
...she can't... → contraction;
It'll take... → contraction
**(9)** The weather → It; Maria → she
**(10)** Just as she suspected, her friends had organised a party for her. *(2nd box)*

### Grammar & Punctuation Test 2E (pp. 32-33)

**(1)** It shows that there is something that the person does not know. *(1st box)*; It shows that the person would like someone else to say something. *(3rd box)*
**(2)** yours
**(3)** could've → could have; they'd → they would
**(4)** whose performance made me cry
**(5)** a noun phrase *(1st box)*
**(6)** Shereen checked the hutch by the shed. *(1st box)*; She hadn't seen him since breakfast. *(4th box)*
**(7)** *Answers will differ, but any correct response must show an understanding that the items in (A) are 'dinosaur model' & 'fossils', and that the items in (B) are 'dinosaur' & 'model fossils'. Example:* (A) shows Pete was looking at a dinosaur model while (B) shows the children were shown model fossils.
**(8)** They run their own business; the hours are long, but it is rewarding. *(3rd box)*
**(9)** yet **OR** but
**(10)** sturdy; reliable; plain

### Grammar & Punctuation Test 3A (pp. 35-36)

**(1)** ...said the fairy sadly;
...said the fairy with sadness.
**(2)** Sherlock Holmes solved the mystery.
**(3)** for
**(4)** some
**(5)** The programme has already started. **OR** The programme has started already.
**(6)** ...before the large... → preposition;
Before she could... → conjunction;
...queue before her. → preposition
**(7)** The Incas held the Festival of the Sun every year. **OR** Every year, the Incas held the Festival of the Sun.
**(8)** when; and; since
**(9)** enough; two; three
**(10)** Deep beneath...ocean floor. It had... hundred years. All that...to change.

### Grammar & Punctuation Test 3B (pp. 38-39)

**(1)** impractical; incomplete; displease
**(2)** alphabetical → adjective; alphabet → noun; alphabetise → verb
**(3)** ...very popular: it had...
**(4)** Jacques
**(5)** Can Rosa see her friends once she finishes her homework? *(2nd box)*; If Rosa finishes her homework, can she see her friends? *(4th box)*
**(6)** ...was overjoyed — positively ecstatic — when she...
**(7)** Fran, whose phone...;
...person who had...;
...number that had...
**(8)** Immediately after the loud boom, all...;
According to local legend, the...
**(9)** ...a hardback's dust...
**(10)** Juanita has had a state-of-the-art laser printer set up in her office. *(4th box)*

### Grammar & Punctuation Test 3.C (pp. 41-42)

**(1)** Our new kitten, whose name is Cuddles, is chasing butterflies in the garden. *(2nd box)*
**(2)** ...South <u>Africa — he's</u> wanted...
**(3)** I'm sure there was a fox in our <u>back</u> garden last night. *(3rd box)*
**(4)** leaves → left; goes → went
**(5)** Trish was unable to make sense of his conduct. *(1st box)*
**(6)** "<u>Did</u>...<u>you?</u>" **OR** '<u>Did</u>...<u>you?</u>'
**(7)** remember *(2nd box)*
**(8)** Where's the... → contraction;
If you've... → contraction;
...the children's... → possession
**(9)** The novel and the film → They; the novel and the film → they
**(10)** We were waiting for Helena when our phones rang. *(3rd box)*

### Grammar & Punctuation Test 3.D (pp. 44-45)

**(1)** It shows that the person is making a statement. *(2nd box)*; It shows that the person is not shouting. *(3rd box)*
**(2)** mine
**(3)** have not → haven't; we will → we'll
**(4)** <u>who sells curious antiques</u>
**(5)** a main clause *(2nd box)*
**(6)** So, he went and sat underneath a bridge. *(2nd box)*; Tuber looked, but he couldn't see anyone near him. *(5th box)*
**(7)** *Answers will differ, but any correct response must show an understanding that the items in (A) are 'cave art' & 'books', and that the items in (B) are 'cave' & 'art books'. Example:* (A) shows Fiona was admiring the cave art while (B) shows tourists were being sold books about art.
**(8)** Veronika's stew was delicious; her guests had to have second helpings. *(1st box)*
**(9)** Unless
**(10)** startled; sudden; screeching

### Grammar & Punctuation Test 3.E (pp. 47-48)

**(1)** What a brilliant person that scientist is *(1st box)*
**(2)** Where are the... → question;
Where the bandits... → statement;
Where all this... → statement;
Where has Diana... → question
**(3)** edit → or; access → ible; pack → age; just → ify
**(4)** ...the <u>wall, crept</u> up the...
**(5)** behave    misbehave *(3rd box)*
**(6)** then /(than); lead /(led); (no one)/ noone
**(7)** Next week, Olga might be visiting her cousins in Carlisle. *(3rd box)*
**(8)** <u>Felicia, who</u> normally avoids rich <u>desserts, enjoyed</u> the...
**(9)** I believe it essential that Danny tell the truth about the events. *(4th box)*
**(10)** Exasperated = irritated

# Spelling Tests: Administration & Marking Guidelines

## Using the Spelling Tests

As with the Grammar & Punctuation tests, these Spelling papers have been designed for you to be able to use them as one, or both, of the following:

- **Quick practice sessions** throughout the school year
- **Tools for targeted exam preparation** during revision sessions before mocks or the actual exams

Similarly, based on how you wish to use the Spelling Tests in this book, you may want to consider the following with regards to how you administer them and award marks as well as how you time them.

Please be aware though that however you decide to use the material, all the **Spelling Tests** in this book <u>are designed to be read out loud</u> to students from **the transcripts** provided in the following pages.

## Administering the Spelling Tests

If you want to use these tests to help prepare your students for the actual KS2 SATs exam and therefore want **to replicate exam conditions as closely as possible**, then please use the following method.

- Before administering each spelling test, read out the following instructions.

    » *Listen carefully to these instructions.*
    » *There are 10 sentences in your test paper. Each sentence has a word missing from it.*
    » *I will first read the missing word on its own. Then, I will read the whole sentence with the missing word in it. Finally, I will read the missing word again on its own.*
    » *I will do this each time for each sentence.*
    » *Listen carefully to the missing word and write it in the space provided in your test paper.*
    » *Make sure you spell the word correctly.*

- Answer any questions the student may have before proceeding with the test.

- In the Transcripts, there are entries such as the one below:

    *Spelling 1: The word is **delighted**.*
    *Sam was **delighted** with his present.*
    *The word is **delighted**.*

- These should be read out to the student in the following manner:

    » *Read out loud "Spelling number 1."*
    » *Read out loud "The word is delighted."*
    » *Read out loud "Sam was delighted with his present."*
    » *Read out loud "The word is delighted."*

- Leave a gap of at least 12 seconds between each spelling.
- At the end, read all 10 sentences out again in order from the beginning.
- Give the student time to change any of their answers if they wish.
- When the test is over, say "This is the end of the test."

## Administering the Spelling Tests Cont.

Alternatively, if you would like **a far less exam-based way of administering the Spelling Tests,** you may wish to **ignore the SATs-specific framework of 'The word is…' statements** and use one (or a combination) of the methods listed below instead. In each of the following, we will continue to use the *Sam was delighted with his present* example to make the differences between the various methods as clear as possible.

Method 1:
- Simply read out the sentence along with the missing word, saying aloud: *Sam was delighted with his present*

Method 2:
- Read out the target spelling first, saying aloud: *delighted*
- Wait for a few seconds
- Then read out the whole sentence, saying aloud: *Sam was delighted with his present*

Method 3:
- Start with a brief statement like: *Spelling Number 1 is delighted*, or *Number 1 is delighted*, or simply *Number 1*
- Wait for a few seconds
- Then read out the whole sentence, saying aloud: *Sam was delighted with his present*

## Timing the Spelling Tests

To reiterate, if your students are actively revising for the KS2 SATs, we recommend that students **try to complete each test within 10 minutes.**

It is, however, **up to you to decide** how much time to give your students.

You may want them to focus solely on their spellings and not want the distraction of the need to answer quickly. On the other hand, you might want your students to become more experienced at dealing with time constraints. If this is the case, set a time limit that you feel is the most constructive for your students.

## Marking the Spelling Tests

As with the Grammar & Punctuation Tests, the guidelines below are to be followed if you wish to stick to the strict government marking scheme of the actual 2023 Spelling Test.

- Each **correctly spelt word** is worth **1 mark**.
- Half marks **are not to be awarded**.
- If a word requires a **capital letter**, **an apostrophe**, or **a hyphen**, these punctuation marks **must be used correctly** by the student **for the mark to be awarded**.
- Spellings that have been written as **two distinct** or **incorrectly hyphenated** words **cannot be accepted**.

Alternatively, you may like a more flexible approach to marking to encourage students. You might want to award half marks in some instances; for example, when a word is spelt correctly, but is missing a necessary capital letter. Once more, this is left up to you.

# Spelling Tests Transcripts ~ 1.A & 1.B

## Spelling Test 1.A (p. 7)

**Spelling 1**: The word is **calendar**.
Kim finds having more than one digital **calendar** annoying.
The word is **calendar**.

**Spelling 2**: The word is **privilege**.
"It is a **privilege** to meet you, sir," said Dr Watson.
The word is **privilege**.

**Spelling 3**: The word is **accompany**.
Greenleaf, the elf, decided to **accompany** Sir Tristram on his quest.
The word is **accompany**.

**Spelling 4**: The word is **definite**.
"I can't get a **definite** answer out of Ola," grumbled her brother.
The word is **definite**.

**Spelling 5**: The word is **soldier**.
Can you guess what the expression 'to **soldier** on' means?
The word is **soldier**.

**Spelling 6**: The word is **communicate**.
Some insects **communicate** with each other by producing noises.
The word is **communicate**.

**Spelling 7**: The word is **bargain**.
Lorenzo always finds a good **bargain** in the sales.
The word is **bargain**.

**Spelling 8**: The word is **system**.
When did you first learn about the solar **system**?
The word is **system**.

**Spelling 9**: The word is **familiar**.
"This street seems **familiar**. Have we been here before?" asked Lola.
The word is **familiar**.

**Spelling 10**: The word is **library**.
I would love to go back in time to visit the first ever **library**.
The word is **library**.

## Spelling Test 1.B (p. 10)

**Spelling 1**: The word is **regular**.
Palm trees had been planted at **regular** intervals along the beach.
The word is **regular**.

**Spelling 2**: The word is **awkward**.
He felt **awkward** as he walked onto the stage.
The word is **awkward**.

**Spelling 3**: The word is **convenience**.
Have you tried to live without the **convenience** of a smart phone?
The word is **convenience**.

**Spelling 4**: The word is **vegetable**.
Serena's favourite dish used to be **vegetable** lasagne.
The word is **vegetable**.

**Spelling 5**: The word is **desperate**.
Terrified by the giants, the villagers were **desperate** to escape.
The word is **desperate**.

**Spelling 6**: The word is **temperature**.
He never likes the **temperature**; it's either too hot or too cold.
The word is **temperature**.

**Spelling 7**: The word is **lightning**.
A flash of **lightning** suddenly lit up the dark room.
The word is **lightning**.

**Spelling 8**: The word is **category**.
The word '**category**' is a synonym for 'group', 'class', or 'set'.
The word is **category**.

**Spelling 9**: The word is **probably**.
Based on its title, that film is **probably** a thriller.
The word is **probably**.

**Spelling 10**: The word is **languages**.
"Are many **languages** spoken in Indonesia?" asked Layla.
The word is **languages**.

# Spelling Tests Transcripts ~ 1.C & 1.D

## Spelling Test 1.C (p. 13)

**Spelling 1**: The word is **height**.
I have no idea what my exact **height** is.
The word is **height**.

**Spelling 2**: The word is **determined**.
Darren is **determined** to learn how to make pastry from scratch.
The word is **determined**.

**Spelling 3**: The word is **thorough**.
A **thorough** review of the company has been ordered.
The word is **thorough**.

**Spelling 4**: The word is **February**.
Loads of my friends have their birthdays in **February**.
The word is **February**.

**Spelling 5**: The word is **interrupt**.
"Don't you DARE **interrupt** me!" hissed the witch.
The word is **interrupt**.

**Spelling 6**: The word is **committee**.
The members of the **committee** argued bitterly for hours.
The word is **committee**.

**Spelling 7**: The word is **extreme**.
The archaeologist took **extreme** care with the glass statuette.
The word is **extreme**.

**Spelling 8**: The word is **average**.
On **average**, how much food does a horse eat a day?
The word is **average**.

**Spelling 9**: The word is **profession**.
By **profession**, his aunt is a data scientist.
The word is **profession**.

**Spelling 10**: The word is **marvellous**.
"How SIMPLY **marvellous** to see you, darling!" drawled the countess.
The word is **marvellous**.

## Spelling Test 1.D (p. 16)

**Spelling 1**: The word is **harass**.
I can never remember how to spell the word '**harass**'.
The word is **harass**.

**Spelling 2**: The word is **century**.
In which **century** do you think tomatoes became popular in Europe?
The word is **century**.

**Spelling 3**: The word is **frequently**.
Parcels and letters are **frequently** delivered to us by mistake.
The word is **frequently**.

**Spelling 4**: The word is **programme**.
"Did you catch last night's cooking **programme**?" inquired Steve.
The word is **programme**.

**Spelling 5**: The word is **tomorrow**.
All I plan to do **tomorrow** is to catch up on some sleep.
The word is **tomorrow**.

**Spelling 6**: The word is **available**.
"Are there any tickets **available** for tonight?" she asked.
The word is **available**.

**Spelling 7**: The word is **dictionary**.
I wonder how often people buy a new **dictionary**.
The word is **dictionary**.

**Spelling 8**: The word is **minute**.
How far can a cheetah run in a **minute**?
The word is **minute**.

**Spelling 9**: The word is **consider**.
"I never thought I would **consider** an ogre a friend," admitted Sir Toby.
The word is **consider**.

**Spelling 10**: The word is **develop**.
Joel hoped his sore throat wasn't going to **develop** into a cough.
The word is **develop**.

# Spelling Tests Transcripts ~ 1.E & 2.A

## Spelling Test 1.E (p. 19)

**Spelling 1**: The word is **twelfth**.
I took part in an egg-and-spoon race and came **twelfth**.
The word is **twelfth**.

**Spelling 2**: The word is **attached**.
Anika is very **attached** to her pet hamsters.
The word is **attached**.

**Spelling 3**: The word is **occupy**.
Bored, Luiz looked around for something to **occupy** him.
The word is **occupy**.

**Spelling 4**: The word is **forty**.
**Forty** winners will be selected at random from the audience.
The word is **forty**.

**Spelling 5**: The word is **physical**.
The twin sisters' **physical** resemblance was quite extraordinary.
The word is **physical**.

**Spelling 6**: The word is **mischievous**.
With **mischievous** grins on their faces, the goblins slunk off.
The word is **mischievous**.

**Spelling 7**: The word is **conscience**.
"You must listen to your **conscience**, child," the kindly queen said.
The word is **conscience**.

**Spelling 8**: The word is **bicycle**.
Paul found an old **bicycle** in the bushes at the end of the garden.
The word is **bicycle**.

**Spelling 9**: The word is **through**.
Trekking **through** the forest, they could hear wolves howling.
The word is **through**.

**Spelling 10**: The word is **quarter**.
It took Zak a **quarter** of an hour to get ready.
The word is **quarter**.

## Spelling Test 2.A (p. 22)

**Spelling 1**: The word is **stomach**.
If he doesn't eat regularly, his **stomach** growls very loudly!
The word is **stomach**.

**Spelling 2**: The word is **difficult**.
Auntie Mabel has never found it **difficult** to get to sleep.
The word is **difficult**.

**Spelling 3**: The word is **variety**.
Iris has travelled to a **variety** of places in South America.
The word is **variety**.

**Spelling 4**: The word is **cemetery**.
Angie refuses to walk past the **cemetery** after dusk.
The word is **cemetery**.

**Spelling 5**: The word is **identity**.
Historians do not yet know the **identity** of the person in the portrait.
The word is **identity**.

**Spelling 6**: The word is **muscle**.
The 'hamstring' is a **muscle** at the back of the thigh.
The word is **muscle**.

**Spelling 7**: The word is **grammar**.
"**Grammar** is SO boring," complained the student.
The word is **grammar**.

**Spelling 8**: The word is **queue**.
Kristen groaned when she saw the **queue** at the box office.
The word is **queue**.

**Spelling 9**: The word is **eight**.
"I can't believe you've won **eight** times in a row!" he exclaimed.
The word is **eight**.

**Spelling 10**: The word is **appreciate**.
"I'd **appreciate** a hand with these suitcases!" yelled Enzo.
The word is **appreciate**.

# Spelling Tests Transcripts ~ 2.B & 2.C

## Spelling Test 2.B (p. 25)

**Spelling 1**: The word is **decide**.
"I can't **decide**," Rafael declared. "You choose for us."
The word is **decide**.

**Spelling 2**: The word is **recent**.
These **recent** events make no sense to any of us.
The word is **recent**.

**Spelling 3**: The word is **community**.
A small **community** of farmers lived in the Arcona Valley.
The word is **community**.

**Spelling 4**: The word is **apparent**.
It is still not **apparent** how serious the situation is.
The word is **apparent**.

**Spelling 5**: The word is **naughty**.
My cousin claims I was very **naughty** as a child.
The word is **naughty**.

**Spelling 6**: The word is **vehicle**.
"What does driving an electric **vehicle** feel like?" asked Stan.
The word is **vehicle**.

**Spelling 7**: The word is **guide**.
The travellers hired a **guide** to lead them through the canyons.
The word is **guide**.

**Spelling 8**: The word is **controversy**.
In 1900, these ideas would have sparked much **controversy**.
The word is **controversy**.

**Spelling 9**: The word is **pronunciation**.
Joe and I always argue over the **pronunciation** of the word 'either'.
The word is **pronunciation**.

**Spelling 10**: The word is **excellent**.
Tamar has an **excellent** memory; it is quite remarkable.
The word is **excellent**.

## Spelling Test 2.C (p. 28)

**Spelling 1**: The word is **recognise**.
I'm not sure I would **recognise** Kevin if I saw him now.
The word is **recognise**.

**Spelling 2**: The word is **often**.
Prince Ali was **often** to be found sitting by the magic fountain.
The word is **often**.

**Spelling 3**: The word is **ancient**.
The **ancient** temples were exceptionally magnificent at sunset.
The word is **ancient**.

**Spelling 4**: The word is **disastrous**.
Extreme weather events can have **disastrous** impacts on cities.
The word is **disastrous**.

**Spelling 5**: The word is **necessary**.
"Is all that shrieking really **necessary**?" Sophia asked irritably.
The word is **necessary**.

**Spelling 6**: The word is **yacht**.
Overnight, the large **yacht** sailed out towards the ocean.
The word is **yacht**.

**Spelling 7**: The word is **favourite**.
Vijay insisted that he didn't have a **favourite** song.
The word is **favourite**.

**Spelling 8**: The word is **certain**.
"Are you **certain** that is the right answer?" Gerald asked.
The word is **certain**.

**Spelling 9**: The word is **occur**.
It did not **occur** to Yonas to check the website.
The word is **occur**.

**Spelling 10**: The word is **guarantee**.
Those manufacturers **guarantee** their products for ten years.
The word is **guarantee**.

# Spelling Tests Transcripts ~ 2.D & 2.E

## Spelling Test 2.D (p. 31)

**Spelling 1**: The word is **foreign**.
Dan claims to speak six **foreign** languages fluently.
The word is **foreign**.

**Spelling 2**: The word is **exaggerate**.
"Why do you **exaggerate** everything?" she asked impatiently.
The word is **exaggerate**.

**Spelling 3**: The word is **interfere**.
Annoyingly, his cousin always seems to **interfere** with our plans.
The word is **interfere**.

**Spelling 4**: The word is **nuisance**.
Carla's younger brother solemnly promised not to be a **nuisance**.
The word is **nuisance**.

**Spelling 5**: The word is **convenient**.
"Is 10 o'clock a **convenient** time for you?" Faisal asked.
The word is **convenient**.

**Spelling 6**: The word is **amateur**.
Our local **amateur** dramatics club puts on several plays a year.
The word is **amateur**.

**Spelling 7**: The word is **remember**.
"Do you **remember** where I agreed to meet Sue?" Tina asked me.
The word is **remember**.

**Spelling 8**: The word is **hindrance**.
While picturesque, the old narrow roads were a **hindrance** to traffic.
The word is **hindrance**.

**Spelling 9**: The word is **recommend**.
"I wouldn't **recommend** the pumpkin soup," whispered the waiter.
The word is **recommend**.

**Spelling 10**: The word is **accident**.
"Arrgh! I've just deleted my files by **accident**," groaned Gita.
The word is **accident**.

## Spelling Test 2.E (p. 34)

**Spelling 1**: The word is **occasion**.
"Is this going to be a formal **occasion**?" Siobhan asked.
The word is **occasion**.

**Spelling 2**: The word is **correspond**.
Years ago, people wrote letters to **correspond** with each other.
The word is **correspond**.

**Spelling 3**: The word is **explanation**.
I was unconvinced by her **explanation** of events.
The word is **explanation**.

**Spelling 4**: The word is **symbol**.
She noticed a curious **symbol** on the old silver coin.
The word is **symbol**.

**Spelling 5**: The word is **especially**.
Justine was **especially** nice to me today; I've no idea why.
The word is **especially**.

**Spelling 6**: The word is **restaurant**.
"I'm NEVER going back to that **restaurant**!" fumed Mario.
The word is **restaurant**.

**Spelling 7**: The word is **opportunity**.
Alma has been given the thrilling **opportunity** to work on a film set.
The word is **opportunity**.

**Spelling 8**: The word is **aggressive**.
He is scared of dogs; it doesn't matter if they are **aggressive** or not.
The word is **aggressive**.

**Spelling 9**: The word is **knowledge**.
The High Priestess was famous for her **knowledge** of medicine.
The word is **knowledge**.

**Spelling 10**: The word is **rhyme**.
I still find the **rhyme** "Thirty days hath September…" useful.
The word is **rhyme**.

# Spelling Tests Transcripts ~ 3.A & 3.B

## Spelling Test 3.A (p. 37)

**Spelling 1**: The word is **address**.
Please include your email **address** on the form.
The word is **address**.

**Spelling 2**: The word is **however**.
You can decorate your room **however** you like.
The word is **however**.

**Spelling 3**: The word is **equip**.
"I will help **equip** you with survival skills," said the instructor.
The word is **equip**.

**Spelling 4**: The word is **existence**.
"I have long wondered about the **existence** of ghosts," he confessed.
The word is **existence**.

**Spelling 5**: The word is **parallel**.
A real-life example of **parallel** lines are the rungs of a ladder.
The word is **parallel**.

**Spelling 6**: The word is **interesting**.
"He never has anything **interesting** to say," she grumbled.
The word is **interesting**.

**Spelling 7**: The word is **collision**.
Frankie narrowly avoided a **collision** with a cyclist.
The word is **collision**.

**Spelling 8**: The word is **Wednesday**.
For some odd reason, **Wednesday** is Ida's favourite day of the week.
The word is **Wednesday**.

**Spelling 9**: The word is **breathe**.
"I can't **breathe** through my blocked nose," complained Willow.
The word is **breathe**.

**Spelling 10**: The word is **sacrifice**.
The woodland elves made many a **sacrifice** to help save the fairies.
The word is **sacrifice**.

## Spelling Test 3.B (p. 40)

**Spelling 1**: The word is **shoulder**.
My baby brother says 'soldier' for '**shoulder**'.
The word is **shoulder**.

**Spelling 2**: The word is **immediately**.
Once the work is done, I'll send it to Eric **immediately**.
The word is **immediately**.

**Spelling 3**: The word is **separate**.
At the crossroads, the two wizards went their **separate** ways.
The word is **separate**.

**Spelling 4**: The word is **therefore**.
"I have, **therefore**, decided to resign," finished the mayor.
The word is **therefore**.

**Spelling 5**: The word is **competition**.
Zane has just taken part in his first science **competition**.
The word is **competition**.

**Spelling 6**: The word is **government**.
"Have you considered a career in local **government**?" he asked her.
The word is **government**.

**Spelling 7**: The word is **particular**.
"Is there a **particular** monument you want to see?" Murphy asked.
The word is **particular**.

**Spelling 8**: The word is **wonderful**.
"I've just made a **wonderful** discovery!" said Una excitedly.
The word is **wonderful**.

**Spelling 9**: The word is **achieve**.
"There is much I wish to **achieve**," the young inventor declared.
The word is **achieve**.

**Spelling 10**: The word is **disappear**.
They watched the sun gradually **disappear** behind the mountains.
The word is **disappear**.

# Spelling Tests Transcripts ~3.C & 3.D

## Spelling Test 3.C (p. 43)

**Spelling 1**: The word is **parliament**.
Did you know that a group of owls is called a '**parliament** of owls'?
The word is **parliament**.

**Spelling 2**: The word is **peculiar**.
"There's a **peculiar** smell coming from the fridge," sniffed Lily.
The word is **peculiar**.

**Spelling 3**: The word is **argument**.
Ben and Jerry have had an **argument** over whose turn it is.
The word is **argument**.

**Spelling 4**: The word is **secretary**.
The manager's **secretary** was unbelievably rude to me.
The word is **secretary**.

**Spelling 5**: The word is **criticise**.
"I haven't come to **criticise**; I've come to help," she said.
The word is **criticise**.

**Spelling 6**: The word is **perhaps**.
If you are concerned, **perhaps** you should call Maggie.
The word is **perhaps**.

**Spelling 7**: The word is **suggest**.
Ivan couldn't **suggest** a single good film to watch.
The word is **suggest**.

**Spelling 8**: The word is **individual**.
"The **individual** who made this mess must clean it up," he said.
The word is **individual**.

**Spelling 9**: The word is **rhythm**.
Aida's sense of **rhythm** makes her an ideal drummer.
The word is **rhythm**.

**Spelling 10**: The word is **signature**.
"Your **signature** is just as illegible as mine!" huffed Suzanne.
The word is **signature**.

## Spelling Test 3.D (p. 46)

**Spelling 1**: The word is **length**.
Lydia found a **length** of rope at the bottom of the chest.
The word is **length**.

**Spelling 2**: The word is **according**.
"**According** to local legend," said Yuki, "that cottage is haunted."
The word is **according**.

**Spelling 3**: The word is **sufficient**.
We believe we have **sufficient** local support for our plans.
The word is **sufficient**.

**Spelling 4**: The word is **environment**.
Unlike Khaled, I can't concentrate in a noisy **environment**.
The word is **environment**.

**Spelling 5**: The word is **ordinary**.
For the dwarves, the day had started like any other **ordinary** day.
The word is **ordinary**.

**Spelling 6**: The word is **persuade**.
Mrs Maher found it easy to **persuade** Kelly to join her for lunch.
The word is **persuade**.

**Spelling 7**: The word is **bruise**.
"Ooh! That's a nasty **bruise**! What happened?" asked Anton.
The word is **bruise**.

**Spelling 8**: The word is **sincere**.
"Do you think his apology was **sincere**?" she wondered.
The word is **sincere**.

**Spelling 9**: The word is **leisure**.
Much of Omar's **leisure** time is spent taking photographs.
The word is **leisure**.

**Spelling 10**: The word is **opposite**.
What do you call a word that has the **opposite** meaning to another?
The word is **opposite**.

# Spelling Tests Transcripts ~ 3.E

## Spelling Test 3.E (p. 49)

**Spelling 1**: The word is **prejudice**.
A synonym for the word '**prejudice**' is 'intolerance'.
The word is **prejudice**.

**Spelling 2**: The word is **actual**.
Our team's **actual** score was much higher than we expected.
The word is **actual**.

**Spelling 3**: The word is **neighbour**.
Last Saturday, our **neighbour** was visited by several loud guests.
The word is **neighbour**.

**Spelling 4**: The word is **conscious**.
"Don't nag!" snapped Ira. "I am **conscious** of the time!"
The word is **conscious**.

**Spelling 5**: The word is **accommodate**.
Our stadium can **accommodate** up to 60,000 spectators.
The word is **accommodate**.

**Spelling 6**: The word is **strength**.
Uncle Gavin claims that chicken soup is the secret of his **strength**.
The word is **strength**.

**Spelling 7**: The word is **relevant**.
Yolanda frequently makes comments that aren't **relevant**.
The word is **relevant**.

**Spelling 8**: The word is **embarrass**.
"I'm sorry! I didn't mean to **embarrass** you!" exclaimed Seth.
The word is **embarrass**.

**Spelling 9**: The word is **curiosity**.
Fran always lets her **curiosity** get the better of her.
The word is **curiosity**.

**Spelling 10**: The word is **complete**.
"That is **complete** and utter nonsense," scoffed Jason.
The word is **complete**.

# 200 Spelling Words, Parts of Speech & Definitions

## Notes to 200 Spelling Words

Please note that **some of the words below can be correctly used in more than one way**.
For example, the word 'run' can be **a verb** (e.g. We run every day) **or a noun** (e.g. She went for a run).
For such words, <u>only one part of speech</u> is noted and relates to the definition given.

In a similar vein, **some of the words below have more than one correct meaning**.
For example, the noun 'exercise' can mean 'physical activity to keep healthy'; it can also mean 'a piece of written work to practise something that is being learnt'.
For such words, a <u>single definition</u> has been given to prevent the list from becoming too long.

All 200 government words are listed in **alphabetical order**.
For your convenience, they have each been labelled **3&4** or **5&6** to indicate which list they are found in.

Where the government list has included **suffixes in brackets after certain words**, like '**critic(ise)**', the list below treats each as a separate entry. Hence, you will find both the words '**critic**' and '**criticise**' and so on.

**Both government lists can be found in a PDF online @**
https://www.gov.uk/government/publications/national-curriculum-in-england-english-programmes-of-study

## Parts of Speech (PoS) Abbreviations

The following abbreviations are used in the list below:

adj. = adjective        det. = determiner       prep. = preposition
adv. = adverb           n. = noun               v. = verb
conj. = conjunction     pl. n. = plural noun

| Word | PoS | Quick Definition | Years |
|---|---|---|---|
| accident | n. | an unfortunate event which happens by chance | 3&4 |
| accidentally | adv. | by chance | 3&4 |
| accommodate | v. | to have enough space for a specific purpose | 5&6 |
| accompany | v. | to go with someone | 5&6 |
| according (to) | prep. | as stated by | 5&6 |
| achieve | v. | to do something successfully | 5&6 |
| actual | adj. | being real | 3&4 |
| actually | adv. | really | 3&4 |

67

# 200 Spelling Words, Parts of Speech & Definitions

| Word | PoS | Quick Definition | Years |
| --- | --- | --- | --- |
| address | v. | to talk to someone | 3&4 |
| aggressive | adj. | being very forceful | 5&6 |
| although | conj. | in spite of | 3&4 |
| amateur | n. | a person who does something for pleasure, not for money | 5&6 |
| ancient | adj. | being very old | 5&6 |
| answer | v. | to reply to someone | 3&4 |
| apparent | adj. | being clear | 5&6 |
| appear | v. | to come into view | 3&4 |
| appreciate | v. | to value something | 5&6 |
| arrive | v. | to reach a place | 3&4 |
| attached | adj. | being joined to something | 5&6 |
| available | adj. | being ready for use | 5&6 |
| average | adj. | being typical | 5&6 |
| awkward | adj. | being difficult & embarrassing | 5&6 |
| bargain | v. | to try to agree on a price of something with someone | 5&6 |
| believe | v. | to accept as true | 3&4 |
| bicycle | n. | a two-wheeled vehicle that you ride | 3&4 |
| breath | n. | a gulp of air | 3&4 |
| breathe | v. | to take in and let out air | 3&4 |
| bruise | v. | to injure without cutting or grazing the skin | 5&6 |
| build | v. | to construct something | 3&4 |
| business | n. | the work that is done to make money | 3&4 |
| busy | adj. | having a lot to do | 3&4 |
| calendar | n. | a chart showing days, weeks and months | 3&4 |

# 200 Spelling Words, Parts of Speech & Definitions

| Word | PoS | Quick Definition | Years |
| --- | --- | --- | --- |
| category | n. | a group of things with similar characteristics | 5&6 |
| caught | v. | grabbed something that had been thrown | 3&4 |
| cemetery | n. | a place where people are buried | 5&6 |
| centre | n. | the middle of something | 3&4 |
| century | n. | a period of one hundred years | 3&4 |
| certain | adj. | being sure about something | 3&4 |
| circle | v. | to go round | 3&4 |
| committee | n. | a group of people chosen to do something specific | 5&6 |
| communicate | v. | to share thoughts with someone | 5&6 |
| community | n. | a group of people living together | 5&6 |
| competition | n. | a contest | 5&6 |
| complete | v. | to finish doing something | 3&4 |
| conscience | n. | a sense of right and wrong | 5&6 |
| conscious | adj. | being aware of | 5&6 |
| consider | v. | to think about something | 3&4 |
| continue | v. | to keep doing something | 3&4 |
| controversy | n. | a public argument involving lots of people and strong opinions | 5&6 |
| convenience | n. | something that makes doing things easier | 5&6 |
| correspond | v. | to be very similar to something else | 5&6 |
| critic | n. | someone who gives an opinion about something | 5&6 |
| criticise | v. | to find fault with something or someone | 5&6 |
| curiosity | n. | a wish to know something | 5&6 |
| decide | v. | to make up your mind about something | 3&4 |
| definite | adj. | being certain or fixed | 5&6 |

69

# 200 Spelling Words, Parts of Speech & Definitions

| Word | PoS | Quick Definition | Years |
|---|---|---|---|
| describe | v. | to say what someone or something is like | 3&4 |
| desperate | adj. | needing something very much | 5&6 |
| determined | adj. | being set on doing something | 5&6 |
| develop | v. | to build up something | 5&6 |
| dictionary | n. | a book of lists of words in alphabetical order with their meanings | 5&6 |
| different | adj. | not being the same | 3&4 |
| difficult | adj. | being hard in some way | 3&4 |
| disappear | v. | to vanish | 3&4 |
| disastrous | adj. | resulting in a lot of damage | 5&6 |
| early | adj. | happening before the expected time | 3&4 |
| earth | n. | the planet on which we live | 3&4 |
| eight | n. | the number that comes after seven | 3&4 |
| eighth | adj. | being number eight in a series | 3&4 |
| embarrass | v. | to make someone feel ashamed | 5&6 |
| enough | det. | being the amount that is needed | 3&4 |
| environment | n. | the natural world | 5&6 |
| equip | v. | to provide things that are needed | 5&6 |
| equipment | n. | the items needed for a certain task | 5&6 |
| equipped | adj. | having all the things that you need | 5&6 |
| especially | adv. | particularly | 5&6 |
| exaggerate | v. | to make something seem greater or smaller than it is | 5&6 |
| excellent | adj. | being extremely good | 5&6 |
| exercise | v. | to do physical activity | 3&4 |
| existence | n. | the state of being alive | 5&6 |

# 200 Spelling Words, Parts of Speech & Definitions

| Word | PoS | Quick Definition | Years |
|---|---|---|---|
| experience | v. | to live through an event | 3&4 |
| experiment | v. | to carry out tests on something | 3&4 |
| explanation | n. | a statement that gives the reasons for something | 5&6 |
| extreme | adj. | being very large or great in degree or quantity | 3&4 |
| familiar | adj. | being known to someone | 5&6 |
| famous | adj. | being well known | 3&4 |
| favourite | adj. | being liked the most | 3&4 |
| February | n. | the second month of the year | 3&4 |
| foreign | adj. | being unfamiliar | 5&6 |
| forty | n. | the number that comes after thirty-nine | 5&6 |
| forward | adv. | moving in the direction a person is facing | 3&4 |
| forwards | adv. | moving ahead | 3&4 |
| frequently | adv. | often | 5&6 |
| fruit | n. | parts of plants that can be eaten such as strawberries | 3&4 |
| government | n. | a group of people having the authority to rule over a country | 5&6 |
| grammar | n. | the rules of a language | 3&4 |
| group | v. | to put several people or things together | 3&4 |
| guarantee | v. | to promise that something will be done | 5&6 |
| guard | v. | to protect someone or something | 3&4 |
| guide | v. | to show someone the way to a place | 3&4 |
| harass | v. | to put pressure on someone | 5&6 |
| heard | v. | became aware of a sound | 3&4 |
| heart | n. | the central part of something | 3&4 |
| height | n. | the measurement of someone or something from top to bottom | 3&4 |

# 200 Spelling Words, Parts of Speech & Definitions

| Word | PoS | Quick Definition | Years |
|---|---|---|---|
| hindrance | n. | a person or thing that is getting in the way of progress | 5&6 |
| history | n. | the study of the past | 3&4 |
| identity | n. | the name of a person or thing | 5&6 |
| imagine | v. | to form a picture in your mind | 3&4 |
| immediate | adj. | happening or being done at once | 5&6 |
| immediately | adv. | straight away | 5&6 |
| important | adj. | having great effect or value | 3&4 |
| increase | v. | to become greater in size or number | 3&4 |
| individual | adj. | being separate | 5&6 |
| interest | v. | to attract the attention of someone | 3&4 |
| interfere | v. | to become involved in a situation without being asked | 5&6 |
| interrupt | v. | to stop the progress of something | 5&6 |
| island | n. | a piece of land surrounded by water | 3&4 |
| knowledge | n. | information learned through experience or education | 3&4 |
| language | n. | a system of words used for communication | 5&6 |
| learn | v. | to gain knowledge | 3&4 |
| leisure | n. | free time for enjoyment | 5&6 |
| length | n. | the measurement of something from one end to the other | 3&4 |
| library | n. | a room or a building where books are kept | 3&4 |
| lightning | n. | a flash of bright light seen in the sky | 5&6 |
| marvellous | adj. | being extremely good | 5&6 |
| material | n. | cloth that clothes can be made from | 3&4 |
| medicine | n. | a substance for treating or preventing a disease | 3&4 |
| mention | v. | to refer to something briefly | 3&4 |

# 200 Spelling Words, Parts of Speech & Definitions

| Word | PoS | Quick Definition | Years |
|---|---|---|---|
| minute | n. | one of the sixty parts that form an hour | 3&4 |
| mischievous | adj. | being naughty, but not meaning to cause harm | 5&6 |
| muscle | n. | body tissue that helps make movement possible in humans and animals | 5&6 |
| natural | adj. | not made or caused by people | 3&4 |
| naughty | adj. | being badly behaved and disobedient | 3&4 |
| necessary | adj. | being needed so that something else can happen | 5&6 |
| neighbour | n. | a person living next door or very near you | 5&6 |
| notice | v. | to become aware of someone or something | 3&4 |
| nuisance | n. | a troublesome person or thing | 5&6 |
| occasion | n. | a special time or event | 3&4 |
| occasionally | adv. | from time to time | 3&4 |
| occupy | v. | to keep a person busy with an activity | 5&6 |
| occur | v. | to happen | 5&6 |
| often | adv. | frequently | 3&4 |
| opportunity | n. | a chance that makes it possible to do something | 5&6 |
| opposite | n. | a thing that is completely different from something else | 3&4 |
| ordinary | adj. | not having any special features | 3&4 |
| parliament | n. | the group of people who have been elected to make laws for the country | 5&6 |
| particular | adj. | being special | 3&4 |
| peculiar | adj. | being different to what you expect | 3&4 |
| perhaps | adv. | possibly, but not certainly | 3&4 |
| persuade | v. | to get someone to do something by giving them a good reason | 5&6 |
| physical | adj. | relating to the body | 5&6 |
| popular | adj. | being liked by people | 3&4 |

73

# 200 Spelling Words, Parts of Speech & Definitions

| Word | PoS | Quick Definition | Years |
| --- | --- | --- | --- |
| position | v. | to put in a particular place | 3&4 |
| possess | v. | to own something | 3&4 |
| possession | n. | an object that someone owns | 3&4 |
| possible | adj. | describing something that can be done | 3&4 |
| potatoes | pl. n. | vegetables with white insides that grow underground | 3&4 |
| prejudice | n. | an opinion that is not reasonable or fair | 5&6 |
| pressure | v. | to try to make someone do something they don't want to do | 3&4 |
| privilege | n. | an advantage that not everyone has | 5&6 |
| probably | adv. | very likely | 3&4 |
| profession | n. | a job that needs specialised education or training | 5&6 |
| programme | n. | a set of planned activities or events | 5&6 |
| promise | v. | to tell someone that you will definitely do something | 3&4 |
| pronunciation | n. | the way we say words | 5&6 |
| purpose | n. | the reason for doing something | 3&4 |
| quarter | n. | one of four equal parts of something | 3&4 |
| question | v. | to ask about something | 3&4 |
| queue | v. | to stand in a line to wait for something | 5&6 |
| recent | adj. | having happened not long ago | 3&4 |
| recognise | v. | to know someone because you have seen them before | 5&6 |
| recommend | v. | to suggest that someone or something is suitable for a certain purpose | 5&6 |
| regular | adj. | always happening at the same time | 3&4 |
| reign | v. | to rule as a monarch, emperor, sultan etc. | 3&4 |
| relevant | adj. | being closely connected with what is happening | 5&6 |
| remember | v. | to be able to keep some information in your memory | 3&4 |

# 200 Spelling Words, Parts of Speech & Definitions

| Word | PoS | Quick Definition | Years |
|---|---|---|---|
| restaurant | n. | a place where you can buy and eat a meal | 5&6 |
| rhyme | n. | a short poem with words at the end of each line that sound the same | 5&6 |
| rhythm | n. | a strong regular beat | 5&6 |
| sacrifice | v. | to give up something you value for a particular reason | 5&6 |
| secretary | n. | an office assistant who deals with emails, meetings, and so on | 5&6 |
| sentence | n. | a group of words that expresses a complete idea | 3&4 |
| separate | v. | to move apart | 3&4 |
| shoulder | n. | what joins a person's arms to the rest of their body | 5&6 |
| signature | n. | a person's name written in their own handwriting | 5&6 |
| sincere | adj. | coming from honest feelings | 5&6 |
| sincerely | adv. | in a truthful way | 5&6 |
| soldier | n. | a person who serves in an army | 5&6 |
| special | adj. | being different in a positive way | 3&4 |
| stomach | n. | the organ in the body where most food is digested | 5&6 |
| straight | adj. | moving in only one direction without any bends | 3&4 |
| strange | adj. | being unusual in some way | 3&4 |
| strength | n. | the power to do something | 3&4 |
| sufficient | adj. | being enough | 5&6 |
| suggest | v. | to put forward an idea | 5&6 |
| suppose | v. | to think something is likely | 3&4 |
| surprise | v. | to cause amazement | 3&4 |
| symbol | n. | a sign used to represent something | 5&6 |
| system | n. | a method for doing something | 5&6 |
| temperature | n. | the amount of heat in a body or a place | 5&6 |

# 200 Spelling Words, Parts of Speech & Definitions

| Word | PoS | Quick Definition | Years |
|---|---|---|---|
| therefore | adv. | for that reason | 3&4 |
| thorough | adj. | being careful to do something completely | 5&6 |
| though | conj. | in spite of the fact that | 3&4 |
| thought | n. | an idea in a person's mind | 3&4 |
| through | prep. | moving from one end to the other | 3&4 |
| twelfth | adj. | one of twelve equal parts of something | 5&6 |
| variety | n. | a collection of different types of things | 5&6 |
| various | adj. | being of different kinds | 3&4 |
| vegetable | n. | parts of plants that can be eaten such as carrots | 5&6 |
| vehicle | n. | a machine (often with wheels) used to move people from place to place | 5&6 |
| weight | n. | the heaviness of a person or thing | 3&4 |
| woman | n. | an adult female human being | 3&4 |
| women | pl. n. | more than one woman | 3&4 |
| yacht | n. | a boat with sails used for racing or pleasure | 5&6 |

# 200 Spelling Words, Parts of Speech & Definitions

| Word | PoS | Quick Definition | Years |
|---|---|---|---|
| restaurant | n. | a place where you can buy and eat a meal | 5&6 |
| rhyme | n. | a short poem with words at the end of each line that sound the same | 5&6 |
| rhythm | n. | a strong regular beat | 5&6 |
| sacrifice | v. | to give up something you value for a particular reason | 5&6 |
| secretary | n. | an office assistant who deals with emails, meetings, and so on | 5&6 |
| sentence | n. | a group of words that expresses a complete idea | 3&4 |
| separate | v. | to move apart | 3&4 |
| shoulder | n. | what joins a person's arms to the rest of their body | 5&6 |
| signature | n. | a person's name written in their own handwriting | 5&6 |
| sincere | adj. | coming from honest feelings | 5&6 |
| sincerely | adv. | in a truthful way | 5&6 |
| soldier | n. | a person who serves in an army | 5&6 |
| special | adj. | being different in a positive way | 3&4 |
| stomach | n. | the organ in the body where most food is digested | 5&6 |
| straight | adj. | moving in only one direction without any bends | 3&4 |
| strange | adj. | being unusual in some way | 3&4 |
| strength | n. | the power to do something | 3&4 |
| sufficient | adj. | being enough | 5&6 |
| suggest | v. | to put forward an idea | 5&6 |
| suppose | v. | to think something is likely | 3&4 |
| surprise | v. | to cause amazement | 3&4 |
| symbol | n. | a sign used to represent something | 5&6 |
| system | n. | a method for doing something | 5&6 |
| temperature | n. | the amount of heat in a body or a place | 5&6 |

# 200 Spelling Words, Parts of Speech & Definitions

| Word | PoS | Quick Definition | Years |
|---|---|---|---|
| therefore | adv. | for that reason | 3&4 |
| thorough | adj. | being careful to do something completely | 5&6 |
| though | conj. | in spite of the fact that | 3&4 |
| thought | n. | an idea in a person's mind | 3&4 |
| through | prep. | moving from one end to the other | 3&4 |
| twelfth | adj. | one of twelve equal parts of something | 5&6 |
| variety | n. | a collection of different types of things | 5&6 |
| various | adj. | being of different kinds | 3&4 |
| vegetable | n. | parts of plants that can be eaten such as carrots | 5&6 |
| vehicle | n. | a machine (often with wheels) used to move people from place to place | 5&6 |
| weight | n. | the heaviness of a person or thing | 3&4 |
| woman | n. | an adult female human being | 3&4 |
| women | pl. n. | more than one woman | 3&4 |
| yacht | n. | a boat with sails used for racing or pleasure | 5&6 |

www.ingramcontent.com/pod-product-compliance
Lightning Source LLC
Chambersburg PA
CBHW081626100526
44590CB00021B/3622